Ezra

Loken Expositional Commentary

———✸✸✸———

Israel P. Loken

www.xulonpress.com

Dedication

---⟨∞∞⟩---

To Kimberley, my loving wife and deepest inspiration

Acknowledgments

———— ✄✄✄ ————

The author of this commentary gratefully acknowledges the following individuals who have made this study possible. I am most deeply indebted to the faculty of Dallas Theological Seminary for providing me with the training necessary to accomplish this task. Of special note is the Department of Bible Exposition, which has provided me with the opportunity to teach seminary students what I have learned. I am also deeply indebted to the administration of the College of Biblical Studies for providing an environment in which I am able to study the Word of God and share with college students what I have learned.

Contents

—∞∞∞—

Foreword

━━━ ⧓ ━━━

The Loken Expositional Commentary series is devoted to the accurate interpretation of the Bible. The AIM of Bible study is to discover the Author's Intended Meaning for his audience. As Terry wrote over one hundred years ago, "In all our private study of the Scriptures for personal edification we do well to remember that the first and great thing is to lay hold of the real spirit and meaning of the sacred writer. There can be no true application, and no profitable taking to ourselves of any lessons of the Bible, unless we first clearly apprehend their original meaning and reference. To build a moral lesson upon an erroneous interpretation of the language of God's Word is a reprehensible procedure. But he who clearly discerns the exact grammatico-historical sense of a passage is the better qualified to give it any legitimate application which its language and context will allow."[1]

In the pursuit of accurate interpretation, the biblical text is examined using the literal, grammatical, historical, cultural, literary hermeneutical system. The literal approach means that each word has a plain, normal meaning. The literal approach allows for figurative language. The grammatical approach seeks to determine the meaning of the text by ascertaining four things: a) the meaning of words (lexicology), b) the form of words (morphology), c) the function of words (parts of speech), and d) the relationships of words (syntax).[2] The historical approach recognizes that each book of the Bible was written to a specific group of readers in a specific historical, geographical situation for a specific reason or purpose. The cultural approach takes into account the beliefs, languages, customs, and practices of the social groups mentioned in the Bible. The literary approach distinguishes the various genres of Scripture, understanding that the style and form of a passage influence how it is to be understood.

The series is written for the informed layperson, student, pastor, and scholar. It is anticipated that each of these groups can benefit from the contents of this book. The individual books are perfect for small group and Sunday School studies. Yet they are also profitable resource tools for pastors and scholars who seek to communicate God's truth to others. It is my sincerest desire that these commentaries will help the reader grow in his knowledge of God's word, in his relationship with God Himself, and in his relationships with others. "The good hand of his God was upon him, for Ezra had set his heart to study the law of the Lord, and to practice it, and to teach His statutes and ordinances in Israel" (Ezra 7:9b-10).

Israel Loken

Introduction: Ezra-Nehemiah or Ezra and Nehemiah?

—⚬⚬⚬—

Preview:

Is it the book of Ezra-Nehemiah or the books of Ezra and Nehemiah? According to the Hebrew Bible it is the book of Ezra-Nehemiah. In our English Bibles it is the books of Ezra and Nehemiah. Which one is right? Does it matter? This chapter will answer these questions.

Introduction

B efore the interpreter can perform a satisfactory analysis of the book of Ezra, it is essential that the boundaries of the narrative be firmly and accurately established. The proper identification of the boundaries of a book and, subsequently, the unity of a book, are crucial elements in literary analysis. One must be aware of the complete text of a narrative before one can effectively examine the literary nature of that composition. Obviously, if a text is not complete the chances of misinterpretation are greatly multiplied. One must also be confident that a single author composed the narrative for that narrative to have a unified message. Multiple authors mean multiple purposes and messages, thus creating a situation where accurate literary analysis is virtually impossible. Ezra's extensive similarities to Nehemiah have called into question its independence from that book, thus leading many scholars to regard the two books as one unified work. As a result, scholarly analysis of Ezra has tended to focus on identifying the various sources which the author used in compiling his historical narrative rather than analyzing the literary text of the book to determine the author's original purpose in writing.

Primarily due to the fact that the books have been preserved in the Masoretic Text as a single book, scholarship has largely assumed that Ezra and Nehemiah should be viewed as a literary unit.[1] Several other factors point to the conclusion that the books are a unit. First, the LXX records Ezra-Nehemiah as a single work entitled Esdras b. Second, the rabbis consider it one book (e.g., *Babylonian Talmud, Baba Batra,* 14b, 15a).[2] Third, the oldest extant Hebrew manuscripts record Ezra-Nehemiah as a single book (e.g., the Aleppo Codex, dated c. A.D. 930). In fact, when the Masoretes calculated the number of verses in the book (685), they did so for the combined Ezra-Nehemiah. They also identified Nehemiah 3:32 as the center of the book. Further indication that the Masoretes viewed the books as a unit lies in the fact that they included their notes on both books after Nehemiah, rather than after each book. Fourth, the earliest church fathers regarded the books as a unit (e.g., Melito of Sardis; Eusebius *Historia Ecclesiastica* 4.26.14). This arrangement also seems to be inferred from Josephus' enumeration of the biblical books (*Contra Apion* 40). It should be noted at this point that each of these arguments arises as a result of the fact that the Hebrew Bible records the two narratives as a literary unit. Fifth, numerous studies have pointed out key stylistic, theological, and epistemological similarities between the two books.[3] Finally, some literary investigations have concluded that structural analysis supports the original unity of the books.[4] While these arguments are certainly compelling, there are nevertheless several reasons why the books should be viewed as separate works.

Nehemiah's Introduction

Nehemiah's book is introduced with the superscription: "The words of Nehemiah the son of Hacaliah." This introduction clearly states that the words contained in the book are the product of Nehemiah himself. Similarly, the extensive use of the first person throughout the book strongly indicates that Nehemiah should be seen as the sole author. The first-person is used in reference to the person of Nehemiah 110 times while Nehemiah is mentioned by name only five times, usually in a general sense (once to identify the author, once in a list, twice to denote the time period "days of Nehemiah," and once to describe the work of Ezra and Nehemiah).

Some scholars have argued that Nehemiah 12:26 and 12:47 indicate that Nehemiah could not have written this section.[5] In these verses the phrase "in the days of Nehemiah" is used to denote that period during which Nehemiah is governor. The use of this phrase, it is argued, indicates that this time period had already passed. Harrison answers this objection: "This is not a serious objection, for the phrase was being used to designate specific eras or periods such as those of Jehoiakim or Zerubbabel. Consistency suggests that the same usage would extend quite naturally to Nehemiah also, since it might have appeared somewhat strange had he employed a different style of reference to the period of his own activity. It should also be noted in passing that these verses are completely irrelevant as far as chronological considerations are concerned, since Nehemiah in his capacity as *tirshatha* or royal commissioner would certainly take priority over others in his own memoirs."[6] It is also possible that Nehemiah shifts to the use of the third person to emphasize the work of others, especially the priesthood. During the early part of the narrative, there is no question that Nehemiah was the instigator of the work. In the latter half of the book, however, Nehemiah seems to be reporting on events as they occur rather than actually instigating those events. Consequently, he appropriately allows other religious leaders to take the foreground in the narrative. It should also be noted that Nehemiah was not present in Jerusalem for the whole period covered in the latter half of the book (cf. Neh. 13:6). It is quite possible that some events may have occurred while he was absent. The author's return to the first person in chapter 13 helps form an inclusio with the first half of the narrative, indicating his authorship of everything in between.

The Repeated List in Ezra 2 and Nehemiah 7
Ezra 2 includes an extensive list of the original returnees. An almost identical list occurs in Nehemiah 7. This repeated list is somewhat redundant if the two books are composed by a single author.[7] Young writes, "The two books are indeed closely related, but the repetition of Ezra 2 in Nehemiah 7:6-70 shows that they were not one originally."[8] Another problem for the common authorship view is the way in which the list is used in each narrative. VanderKam explains,

> In Ezra one reads, 'When the seventh month came and the sons of Israel were in the towns, the people gathered as one man to Jerusalem' [Ezra 3:1]. It then continues with events of the seventh month — the episode of Joshua, Zerubbabel and construction of the altar during Cyrus's reign (therefore between 538 and 530). The parallel in Nehemiah reads, 'And when the seventh month had come, the children of

Israel were in their towns. And all the people gathered as one man into the square before the Water Gate . . .' [Neh. 7:73b-8:1a]. The book then continues with what happened in the seventh month mentioned in it: the reading of the law by Ezra which occurred no earlier than the twentieth year of Artaxerxes (445 or perhaps somewhat later). There is, therefore, a gap of about 90 years between the events of the seventh month in the two books, although the reference to the seventh month is quoted from the same document in each. If the same editor inserted the list into both Ezra 2 and Nehemiah 7, then he would be interpreting the seventh month of the text in one case to refer to a year in Cyrus's reign and in the other to a year in Artaxerxes' reign—a sizable historical blunder.[9]

If Ezra and Nehemiah are regarded as independent literary accounts written by different authors, then the recurring list would not present an imposing problem for the interpreter. Each author simply includes this extensive list because it suits their individual purposes. Ezra uses the list to identify the various groups and individuals who returned in the time of Cyrus while Nehemiah uses the list as the basis for his effort to repopulate the city of Jerusalem. Kraemer elaborates, "The list in Ezra is introduced simply by identifying those included as the ones who returned. But it is followed by speaking of those who came to the house of the LORD in Jerusalem and volunteered to support the rebuilding project (vv. 68-69); the return leads to rebuilding. In contrast, in Nehemiah the list is framed in such a way as to make clear that return leads to rebuilding and repopulation of the city (see 7:4-5 and 69-71), where 'the work' for which donations are made is, given the context, clearly the rebuilding and repopulation effort."[10] Obviously, the repeated list strongly argues for the original separation of the books.

The Omission of Ezra's Activities in Nehemiah 1-7

Another argument which favors the independence of the books is the fact that Nehemiah 1-7 makes no mention of Ezra's activities. While this is admittedly an argument from silence, it nevertheless poses many problems for scholars who hold to the unity of the books. Since Ezra is the main character in the second half of his book, one would assume that he would remain a key character throughout Nehemiah. However, there is no mention of Ezra during Nehemiah's building narrative. One would expect that Nehemiah would seek out Ezra immediately upon entering Jerusalem. One would further expect that Nehemiah would ask for Ezra's aid in building the walls of the city, especially when internal problems arose. This omission, however, can be easily explained if separate authors wrote the books, for Ezra does not appear in Nehemiah until it serves Nehemiah's purpose.

Furthermore, the accounts characterizing Ezra differ radically between the two books. In the book of Ezra, he is introduced as both a priest and a scribe, accompanied by a lengthy and detailed genealogical pedigree (7:1-6). Throughout the narrative, it is Ezra's priestly concerns which dominate as he is concerned with the temple and the religious cult. He is also concerned about the purity of those who worship in the temple as we see in the matter of intermarriages among the people. Kraemer rightly observes, "In the book of Ezra, Ezra is a well-connected priest whose exclusive concern is the strengthening and purification of the cult. His primary activity involves the elimination of intermarriages, an offense that is newly and uniquely described in priestly terms. As befits the emphasis of the book as a whole, Ezra is a man of the priesthood."[11]

The portrait of Ezra in the book of Nehemiah is somewhat different. Here Ezra is related exclusively in the third person and is restricted primarily to chapter eight, though he does make a ceremonial appearance in chapter twelve. While

Ezra is introduced as both a priest and scribe (Neh. 8:1-2), he functions exclusively as a scribe throughout the narrative. In fact, Ezra's other introductions demonstrate that he is regarded primarily as a scribe in the book of Nehemiah. Four times he is spoken of as a scribe alone (Neh. 8:1, 4, 13; 12:36), twice he is named as both a scribe and priest (Neh. 8:9; 12:26), while only in the one passage is he described simply as a priest (Neh. 8:2). His priestly pedigree, so crucial in Ezra (cf. 7:1-5), is completely ignored. Nowhere do we see Ezra performing ritual sacrifices or other priestly functions. He devotes himself to the public reading of Torah and the instruction of the people. Noting this striking contrast, Kraemer concludes, "Thus, the Ezra remembered in Ezra is not the Ezra known in Nehemiah. In Ezra, Ezra is a priest, a man concerned with the cult and its purity, while in Nehemiah he is a scribe, a man of the book, who is entirely unconcerned with the Temple or sacrifices. These are two different Ezras, the one bearing little relationship to the other. The disparate portraits do, however, bear powerful relationship with the ideological bents of the books in which they appear."[12] These vastly different portraits of the character of Ezra throughout the narratives strongly point to the original separation of the books.

Stylistic and Linguistic Differences

A stylistic and linguistic analysis of the two books supports independent authorship. First, Ezra usually writes in first person in Ezra while he is referred to in the third person in Nehemiah. This poses quite a problem if one views Ezra as the author of both books. Second, Ezra uses Aramaic and Hebrew in composing his narrative while Nehemiah uses only Hebrew. While this is admittedly an argument from silence, the question as to why there is no Aramaic in Nehemiah must be addressed. Third, Nehemiah tends to include short prayers while Ezra records lengthy prayers. Fourth, both

Ezra and Nehemiah refer to the temple as the "house of God" (Hebrew, *bet elohim*; e.g., Ezra 3:8; Neh. 12:40), but Ezra alone calls it the "house of the Lord" (Hebrew, *bet yahweh*; e.g., 3:11). Fifth, Ezra routinely employs the divine title "God of Israel" (Hebrew, *elohim yisrael*; 1:3; 3:2; 4:1, 3; 5:1; 6:14, 22; 7:6, 15; 9:4, 15) while it is not attested in Nehemiah. Sixth, though Sukkot is observed in both books, Ezra regards it as a holiday of sacrifices, neglecting to even mention booths, while in Nehemiah it is a holiday of booths and there is no mention of sacrifices. While each of these arguments is insufficient to prove independent authorship, the collective weight of these stylistic differences lends support to the independent authorship view.

Theological Differences

The main focus of the book of Ezra is the restoration of the temple and its cult. The book is built upon priestly concerns. Ezra 6:14 supplies the reader with a succinct, yet comprehensive, thematic statement for the entire book. The people, represented by their elders, successfully complete the rebuilding project through the motivation of the prophets under the protection of the Persian sovereigns. Many scholars who view the books of Ezra and Nehemiah as a unit have incorrectly made this the thematic statement for the collective work, thereby transferring the place of God from the temple to the city and downplaying the role of God's chosen leader in Nehemiah.[13] However, it is clear that Nehemiah maintains a strong distinction between the house of God and the city of Jerusalem (e.g., Neh. 6:10; 8:16; 10:32-39; 11:11, 16, 22; 13:4, 7, 9, 11, 14). Furthermore, rather than Nehemiah's role as leader being diminished throughout the book of Nehemiah, it is actually magnified, even to the extent that many contemporary expositors believe the book to be a manual for leadership principles.[14]

Historical Opinion

At least by the time of Origen (A.D. 185-253) some held that Ezra and Nehemiah should be viewed as separate. Origen was the first to divide the books into two and regarded the books as First and Second Ezra (Eusebius, *Historia Ecclesiastica* 6.25.2). Jerome (A.D. 342-420) introduced the division into the Vulgate, entitling the books "Book of Ezra" and "Book of Nehemiah." A Hebrew manuscript dated A.D. 1448 adopted the division and it was similarly utilized by the Bomberg Bible in A.D. 1525. The books remained divided thereafter in most printed editions. Following this line of evidence, Kraemer rightly concludes, "Whatever the antiquity of such an opinion, its wisdom has to be weighed seriously."[15]

Conclusion

While Ezra and Nehemiah record consecutive historical periods, they do so from significantly different perspectives. After reviewing the evidence, it must be concluded that Ezra and Nehemiah should not be regarded as a single unified work. Several arguments have been presented to demonstrate that the books should be regarded as separate (i.e., Nehemiah's introduction, the repeated list in Ezra 2 and Nehemiah 7, the omission of Ezra's activities in Nehemiah 1-7, stylistic differences, theological differences, and historical opinion). The collective weight of these arguments is overwhelming.

Study Questions

1. Why do many scholars view the books of Ezra and Nehemiah as one book?
2. In your opinion, what is the most convincing argument for regarding the books of Ezra and Nehemiah as one book?

3. Why does Nehemiah switch between first person and third person narration?
4. The list of Ezra 2 is repeated in what chapter of Nehemiah?
5. How does the portrait of Ezra differ between the two books?
6. What are some of the stylistic differences between the two books?
7. Who was the first Church Father to divide Ezra-Nehemiah into two books?
8. In your opinion, what is the most convincing argument for separating Ezra-Nehemiah into two books?

Chapter 1
Introductory Matters for Ezra

Preview:
The book of Ezra describes the fulfillment of the Lord's promise to return His people to the land of Israel after their exile in Babylon. The easiest way for the Lord to accomplish this task would have been to simply raise up a Babylonian king who was sympathetic to the plight of the Jews. Instead, the Lord raises up an entire nation who was sympathetic to the plight of the Jews and uses them to right the wrongs committed by the Babylonians. The Lord's ability to manipulate the most powerful kings on earth to serve His purposes demonstrates His divine sovereignty.

The book of Ezra is one of the most significant books in the Hebrew Bible. It describes the fulfillment of the Lord's promise to return His people to their land after seventy years of exile in Babylon. Throughout the book the Lord is seen as completely sovereign, stirring up the hearts of the key characters to act as He wants them to act. The

Lord is pictured as sovereign even over the most powerful nations on earth as He raises up the Persians to reverse the wrongs committed by the Babylonians.

The book of Ezra also describes the efforts of the Jewish remnant to restore their cultic worship of Yahweh. This remnant is sincere in their efforts to please God; however, their devotion is affected by the apostasy of their age. When the rebuilding efforts do not go smoothly, they abandon the work. When they are attracted to foreign women, they abandon their Jewish wives and marry foreigners. In each case, the Lord raises up spiritual leaders to inform the remnant of their apostasy. Haggai and Zechariah are instrumental in getting the nation to finish the temple while Ezra is used to purify the land of the ungodly marriages. In both cases the nation responds with immediate repentance.

While this repentance was genuine and immediate, it was not long-lasting. The nation will soon begin the task of rebuilding the walls of the city only to halt the work when opposition strikes. The nation's resolve to separate from foreigners only lasts a few years as Nehemiah reveals that the remnant's practice of intermingling with their foreign neighbors continued in his day. Thus, the story of Ezra is one of finished business (temple) and unfinished business (complete restoration, spiritual and physical purity). The unfinished business of Ezra is completed in Nehemiah, a fact that explains why the books were originally joined in the Hebrew Bible.

Author and Date

The author of the book is the scribe Ezra. As a scribe, Ezra was well qualified to write this book. He had likely been educated in the Persian courts, perhaps even serving as one of the royal scribes of King Artaxerxes. If he was a scribe in the court of Artaxerxes it would account for his apparent relationship with the king (cf. 7:6, 21). Ezra's position as scribe allowed him the time needed to effectively study the law of the Lord.

Ezra was also a priest. This fact explains his interest in the temple, the house of God, as well as the sacrificial system. Additionally, this fact provided Ezra with the God-given authority to teach the statutes and ordinances of the Lord to Israel. As a priest, Ezra could take the necessary steps to correct the spiritual condition of the remnant, including commanding those in mixed marriages to separate from their wives.

Ezra was probably somewhere in his forties when he returned to the land in 458 B.C. This would have allowed enough time for his remarkable skills as a scribe to have become noticeable (cf. 7:6, 11). Ezra could not have been much older than this since he was still living fourteen years later when Nehemiah returned to the land in 444 B.C. (cf. Neh. 8:1). It is likely that he died before Nehemiah returned to Babylon in 432 B.C. One would assume that if Ezra was still alive, the reforms of Nehemiah recorded in Nehemiah 13 would have been dealt with by the scribe during Nehemiah's absence.

The last historical event referred to in the book is the reading of the copy of the decree of King Artaxerxes in 4:23. The exact date of this decree cannot be ascertained, though it must have been written between 458 B.C. (the date of Ezra's return to Jerusalem referred to in 4:12) and 444 B.C. (the date of Nehemiah's return to Jerusalem and subsequent rebuilding of the walls of the city). One would assume that Ezra would have wanted to begin work on the walls of the city immediately upon his return so a date closer to 458 B.C. is to be preferred. As a result, the book could have been written as early as 455 B.C.

Audience and Purpose

The book of Ezra was written to the Jews of the postexilic community living in the region of Judea in the mid fifth century B.C. The ancestors of these Jews had returned with Sheshbazzar in 538 B.C. It was now almost a hundred years since that original return. It was well over fifty years since the temple had been rebuilt in 515 B.C. Little had been accomplished since the rebuilding of the temple. A good portion of the recipients had returned with Ezra in 458 B.C. Both the new returnees and the descendants of the original returnees were in need of hope.

The only hope for the nation lay in the fact that God had promised to bless them if they were obedient to the covenant He had given them. The formula had been provided in Deuteronomy 30:1-10. In that passage, the Lord had promised to restore His people from captivity, have compassion on them, and gather them from all the peoples where He had scattered them (Deut. 30:3). The Lord further promised to bring them into the land that their fathers had possessed and prosper them abundantly in all the work of their hands, in the offspring of their cattle, and in the produce of their ground (Deut. 30:5, 9). However, these promises were conditional upon the obedience of the nation. The Lord would do all these things if the nation would obey the Lord to keep His commandments and statutes which are written in the book of the law and turn to the Lord with all their heart and soul (Deut. 30:10).

The book of Ezra is a record of the initial fulfillment of this covenant. The Lord had fulfilled His promise to restore His people from captivity and gather them from the lands to which they had been scattered. He had fulfilled His promise to bring them into the land which their fathers had possessed. However, the Lord had not prospered them abundantly. This was due to the disobedience of the nation. Even though the Lord had given them the ability and resources to rebuild His temple, the exiles had stopped working on the project because of the opposition of their neighbors. As a result, the Lord raised up the prophets Haggai and Zechariah to encourage the remnant to complete the project. The remnant had further disobeyed the Lord by failing to follow His commandments concerning intermarriage with foreigners. As a result, the Lord brought them Ezra the scribe and priest. Ezra showed the remnant the error of their ways and took steps to eliminate the sin from the nation, calling on the guilty parties to divorce their ungodly wives. The key verse of the book is Ezra 9:12, "So now do not give your daughters to their sons nor take their daughters to your sons, and never seek their peace or their prosperity, that you may be strong and eat the good things of the land and leave it as an inheritance to your sons forever." The sin mentioned in this verse is the one specifically addressed by Ezra but it could really have been any sin. The point of the verse is this. Be obedient so that you can receive the blessings promised to you by the Lord forever. The book of Ezra is essentially a call to the postexilic community to be obedient to the Lord so that they can experience the blessings promised to them.

Historical Setting
The events of the book of Ezra take place between 538 B.C. and roughly 455 B.C. Throughout this entire period, the Persians dominated world events as the Persian Empire was at its peak. The region of Judea was simply part of Trans-Euphrates, one of the satrapies in the Persian Empire. The Jews were not autonomous but were governed by the official representatives of the Persian kings. The fortunes of the Jews were dictated by the decisions of foreign kings living more than a thousand miles from the Promised Land. In light of this, it becomes necessary to briefly review the Persian kings of this period.

The founder of the Persian Empire was Cyrus the Great. Cyrus was the son of Cambyses I, a Persian, and Mandane, the daughter of Astyages, king of the Medes. Cyrus became king of the Persians in 559 B.C. and was originally a vassal of King Astyages. Cyrus led a successful revolt against Astyages in 550 B.C. The final battle between the Medes and the Persians took place in the plain of Pasargadae. Cyrus' victory was assured when he was aided by the defection of Astyages' own men. To commemorate his victory, Cyrus built the city of Pasargadae which was soon to become his capital.

Having defeated the Medes, Cyrus embarked on a mission to conquer the known world. His first goal was to solidify his empire, which he accomplished by subduing Lydia and India. His next goal was to defeat the Babylonians. The Babylonians were at this time in a state of turmoil due to the fact that their king Nabonidus was in exile at Teima in Arabia because of his allegiance to the moon god Sin. His son Belshazzar served as ruler in Babylon. Cyrus, who had earlier allied himself with the Babylonians against the Medes, took advantage of the turmoil in Babylon and marched against the city. In 539 B.C., the Persians, under the command of Gubaru,[1] laid siege to the great city of Babylon. Herodotus records that the Persians gained entrance into the city by diverting the Euphrates River (*Histories* 1.191). The city fell on October 12, 539 B.C. with nominal resistance. Belshazzar was killed during or shortly after the battle while Nabonidus was eventually captured and sent into exile to Carmania.

Two and a half weeks later, on October 29, Cyrus himself triumphantly marched into the great city of Babylon, appearing more like a liberator than a conqueror. He forbade destruction and immediately issued an edict allowing all captive peoples to return to their respective homelands. This benevolent foreign policy allowed the Jews to return to Jerusalem under the leadership of Sheshbazzar with the blessing of the king. Cyrus continued to build and solidify his empire until his death in 530 B.C. at the hands of the Massagetae, at which time his son Cambyses II inherited the throne.

Cambyses II was able to secure his control over the throne of Persia by killing his brother Smerdis. The most significant event of the relatively brief reign of Cambyses was his conquest of Egypt in 525 B.C. The Persian armies invaded Egypt and routed the Egyptians at Pelusium. With the Egyptian army defeated, the Persians immediately moved to capture Memphis, the key city in Lower Egypt. Following the fall of Memphis, the rest of Egypt quickly yielded to the Persian armies. Cambyses remained in Egypt for three years, during which time he invaded Ethiopia and was repelled. Cambyses died in the spring of 522 B.C. in the region of Syria. He was on his way home to Persia after learning of a coup d'etat when he accidentally stabbed himself in the thigh while mounting his horse. The wound developed gangrene and Cambyses died three weeks later without leaving an heir.

Following the death of Cambyses, a man named Gaumata usurped the throne and attempted to pass himself off as Smerdis, the murdered brother of Cambyses. In an effort to win over the populace, Gaumata pronounced exemption from taxes and obligatory military service for three years. The ruse was exposed by Phaedyme, the daughter of Otanes, when she discovered that Gaumata's ears had been cut off, a punishment that never would have been committed on the real Smerdis. Darius, a distant cousin of Cambyses, and six nobles formed a coalition to overthrow Gaumata. The coalition managed to assassinate Gaumata in Media on September 29, 522 B.C.

Darius the Great gained the Persian throne in 522 B.C. following the assassination of Gaumata. The father of Darius was Hystaspes, the satrap of Parthia. Darius served at the side of Cambyses as an officer in the ranks of the Immortals, an elite force of ten thousand royal soldiers. Since Darius was not an obvious heir, revolts erupted throughout the Persian Empire. It took nineteen different battles and a little more than a year, but Darius finally succeeded in solidifying his throne.[2] It was during the reign of Darius that the Jews were able to finish building the temple thanks to the motivation of the prophets Haggai and Zechariah. Darius proved to be an extraordinary administrator, implementing far-reaching reforms. Perhaps chief among these was the standardization of coinage, weights, and measures, thus facilitating trade and commerce. He also instituted a system of taxation and reorganized the government of the Persian Empire. Another significant measure taken by Darius was to move the capital of the Persians to Susa where he erected a magnificent palace, referred to in Nehemiah as the "citadel of Susa" (1:1).

Unfortunately, Darius proved a less than stellar military commander. He had some early successes in his military endeavors (e.g., northwestern India, the coastland between the Bosporus and the Grecian state of Thessaly, Thrace, Macedonia), but that would change with his ill-fated decisions to invade Greece. His initial invasion against the Greeks occurred in 493 B.C. This invasion force never even made it to the Grecian mainland because its fleet was destroyed by a storm off Mount Athos in northern Greece. Darius' second, more famous, invasion of Greece took place in 490 B.C. The Persian fleet attacked the coast of Greece, taking the city of Eretria after a week-long siege. The Persians then sailed to the Bay of Marathon where they disembarked and prepared to attack Athens. In one of the most significant battles in history, the Persians were defeated at Marathon by the Athenians. The remaining Persian army refused to give up and attempted to surprise the city of Athens by boarding their ships and sailing around the southern tip of Attica. Thanks to a 26-mile race by a messenger and an all-night march by the weary Athenian army, the city of Athens was protected. The Persians, seeing the Athenian army in battle formation at the harbor of Athens, finally admitted defeat and sailed away. Technically, Darius did not accompany his troops in either invasion. The armies were led by his generals. Although Darius made plans to personally lead his men in a third invasion of Greece, he was never able to quench the rebellions he faced in Egypt. After a long and prosperous reign, Darius died at Persepolis in November of 486 B.C. at the age of sixty-four.

Xerxes, the son of Darius, ascended to the throne at the age of thirty-two. His mother was Atossa, the daughter of Cyrus. The name Xerxes means "he who rules over men." Xerxes is well known in biblical history as the king who chose Esther to be his queen. He is mentioned only in passing in the book of Ezra (4:6). Xerxes, like his father Darius, is notorious in secular history primarily for an ill-fated invasion of Greece. In 481 B.C., he took an army of 200,000 men and hundreds of warships to Greece to avenge his father's defeat at Marathon in 490 B.C. Without a doubt, the troops of Xerxes comprised the largest army and navy ever assembled in antiquity. Initially, Xerxes enjoyed considerable success when the badly divided Greek city-states were unable to achieve an effective coalition.[3] The tide began to turn when the Spartans met this massive invasion force with fierce resistance at the battle of Thermopylae, fighting to the last man. The ill fortune continued for the Persians as their vast navy was destroyed in the battle of Salamis. Xerxes blamed the defeat on his Phoenician and Egyptian mercenaries, accusing them of cowardice. As a result, these mercenaries abandoned him and returned to their homelands. Xerxes himself left for Persia, leaving his armies under the command of Mardonius. Mardonius suffered a series of setbacks until losing his life in the battle of Plataea. The Persians finally admitted defeat with their loss at Mycale in 479 B.C. After a twenty-one year reign, Xerxes was assassinated by Artabanus, a powerful courtier and captain of the royal bodyguard, in 465 B.C. The empire soon fell into the hands of Artaxerxes. Artaxerxes, whose name means "having a kingdom of justice," was the third son of Xerxes and Amestris, the Ahasueras and Vashti of the book of Esther. Artaxerxes managed to kill Artabanus and murder his older brother Darius, the rightful heir to the Persian throne. He then defeated his other brother Hystaspes in battle in the region of Bactria. Artaxerxes, whose first reignal year is reckoned from April 13, 464 B.C.,[4] enjoyed a rather lengthy reign, eventually dying of natural causes in 424 B.C. The returns of both Ezra and Nehemiah took place during his reign.

Outline
I. The Jews Return to Jerusalem (1:1-2:70)
   A. The Opportunity to Return (1:1-11)
      1. The Decree of Cyrus (1:1-4)
      2. The Support of the Neighbors (1:5-6)
      3. The Support of Cyrus (1:7-11)
   B. The Roster of Returnees (2:1-70)
      1. The Leaders of the Return (2:1-2a)
      2. The List of Those with Proof of Ancestry (2:2b-58)
      3. The List of Those without Proof of Ancestry (2:59-63)
      4. The Sum Total of Returnees (2:64-67)
      5. The People Return to Their Cities (2:68-70)
II. The Jews Rebuild Their Temple (3:1-6:22)
   A. The Building of the Altar (3:1-6)
      1. The Nation Gathers in Jerusalem (3:1)
      2. The Altar Rebuilt (3:2-3)
      3. The Nation Celebrates the Feast of Booths (3:4)

A. The Introduction of Ezra the Scribe (7:1-10)
   1. Ezra's Genealogy (7:1-5)
   2. Ezra's Return to Jerusalem (7:6-9)
   3. Ezra's Ministry (7:10)
B. Ezra's Commission from King Artaxerxes (7:11-28)
   1. The Introduction to the Letter (7:11)
   2. The King's Permission (7:12-14)
   3. The King's Provision (7:15-20)
   4. The King's Orders for the Treasurers (7:21-24)
   5. The King's Orders for Ezra (7:25-26)
   6. The Thanksgiving of Ezra (7:27-28)
C. Ezra's Journey to Jerusalem (8:1-36)
   1. The Roster of Returnees (8:1-14)
   2. The Search for Levites (8:15-20)
   3. The Spiritual Preparation (8:21-23)
   4. The Treasure Bearers (8:24-30)
   5. Ezra's Arrival in Jerusalem (8:31-36)
D. The Problem of Mixed Marriages (9:1-10:44)
   1. Ezra Learns of the Apostasy (9:1-4)
   2. Ezra's Prayer (9:5-15)
      a. The Time of the Prayer (9:5)
      b. The Sins of the Nation (9:6-7)
      c. The Faithfulness of God (9:8-9)
      d. The Words of the Prophets (9:10-12)
      e. The Future of the Remnant (9:13-15)
   3. The Solution to the Problem (10:1-8)
      a. The Approach of the People (10:1)
      b. The Recommendation of Shecaniah (10:2-4)
      c. The Proclamation to Assemble in Jerusalem (10:5-8)
   4. The Assembly in Jerusalem (10:9-44)
      a. Ezra's Call for Repentance (10:9-11)
      b. The Response of the Assembly (10:12-15)
      c. The Investigation Hearings (10:16-17)

d. The List of Those Guilty of Intermarriage
   (10:18-44)

Study Questions
1. Who is the author of the book of Ezra?
2. What are the two occupations of Ezra?
3. What two prophets are instrumental in getting the remnant to rebuild the temple?
4. What is the key verse of the book of Ezra?
5. What empire is in control during the entire historical period described in the book of Ezra?
6. Who was the first king of this empire?
7. On what date did this empire conquer the city of Babylon?
8. Who attempted to pass himself off as Smerdis?
9. The battle of Marathon occurred in what year?

Chapter 2
The Lord Stirs the Spirit of Cyrus
Ezra 1:1

Preview:
The first verse of Ezra records the fulfillment of two of the most amazing prophecies in history. First, the Lord, speaking through the prophet Isaiah, demonstrated His sovereignty by predicting the rise of Cyrus almost 200 years before he came to power. Second, the Lord, this time speaking through the prophet Jeremiah, further demonstrated His sovereignty by predicting that the nation would remain in exile for seventy years.

The First Year of Cyrus (1:1a)

The book of Ezra begins with the phrase "Now in the first year of Cyrus king of Persia." The word "now" is the Hebrew connective *waw* and is usually translated "and." It is quite common for Semitic historical books to begin with *waw*. In fact, the only historical books of the Old Testament which do not begin with *waw* are Genesis, Deuteronomy, Chronicles, and Nehemiah. This introduction signifies that the book should be read as a historical narrative. The author obviously wishes to connect the events of this book with those already recorded concerning the history of the Jews. As a result, the book of Ezra more naturally follows the book of Kings rather than the book of Chronicles. The book of Chronicles is better seen as a work of propaganda rather than as a historical narrative.

The first year of Cyrus king of Persia is 539/538 B.C. This date is a reference to the first year in which he was king over all of Mesopotamia, including Babylon. Cyrus the Great was the founder of the Persian Empire. He was the son of Cambyses I, a Persian, and Mandane, the daughter of Astyages, king of the Medes. Cyrus became king of the Persians in 559 B.C. Cyrus was originally a vassal of King Astyages, however, he led a successful revolt against Astyages in 550 B.C. Having defeated the Medes, Cyrus embarked on a mission to conquer the known world. He solidified his empire by subduing Lydia and India. His most notable conquest was the city of Babylon. Cyrus, who had earlier allied himself with the Babylonians against the Medes, took advantage of turmoil in Babylon and marched against the city. In 539 B.C., the Persians laid siege to the great city of Babylon. The city fell on October 12, 539 B.C. with nominal resistance. This date marks the beginning of the first year of Cyrus referred to in 1:1.

Cyrus continued to build and solidify his empire until his death in 530 B.C., at which time his son Cambyses II inherited the throne. The inscription on the tomb of Cyrus reads, "Mortal! I am Cyrus, son of Cambyses, who founded the Persian Empire, and was Lord of Asia. Grudge me not, then, my monument" (*Arrian* 6.29). The rise of Cyrus is one of the most amazing fulfillments of biblical prophecy. Identifying him by name, Isaiah had prophesied the coming of Cyrus almost 200 years before he came to power, revealing that Cyrus will be used by the Lord to initiate the rebuilding of the city of Jerusalem, including the temple (Isa. 44:28; 45:1).

As "king of Persia," Cyrus ruled over the Persians. The Persians were an Indo-European tribe who entered the Iranian plateau about 1400 B.C. They systematically grew in size and power over the next eight hundred years. Cyrus himself is regarded as the founder of the Persian Empire in power during the time of Ezra. The various kings of this vast empire were known as Achaemenians, after an eponymous ancestor, Achaemenes (c. 700 B.C.).[1] From the reign of Cyrus until the time of Alexander the Great, the Achaemenians were able to build one of the largest and most successful of all ancient empires. At its peak, the empire stretched from the Hellespont in the northwest and the Nile in the southwest to the Indus in the east.[2] Economically speaking, the Persian Empire was largely made up of nomadic pastoralists.[3]

The Fulfillment of Jeremiah's Prophecy (1:1b)

In his first year, Cyrus issued a proclamation allowing the Jews to return to their homeland to rebuild the temple in Jerusalem. This event is said to "fulfill" the words spoken by Jeremiah. The reference here is to Jeremiah 25:11-12 and 29:10 where Jeremiah predicts seventy years of captivity for the Jews. It is to these same passages that Daniel appeals while praying for the Lord's mercy in Daniel 9:2. These verses would have been well-known to the exiles since the nation's hopes for deliverance from bondage rested upon the Lord's promise through Jeremiah.

A question arises at this point as to the exact nature of the fulfillment of Jeremiah's prophecy. There are two alternatives for the reckoning of Jeremiah's seventy years. First, the time can be seen as referring to the initial deportation of the Jews in 605 B.C. to the first return of the Jews in roughly 538 B.C. Second, the time can be reckoned from the destruction of the city, and consequently the temple, in 586 B.C. until the temple is completely rebuilt in 515 B.C.

While both alternatives are possible, the first view makes better sense for the following reasons. First, the emphasis of the prophecy is on the exile of the nation, not on the state of the temple. Jeremiah 25:11 says "these nations shall serve the king of Babylon seventy years." The nation first begins to serve Nebuchadnezzar in 605 B.C. It is difficult to see the nation serving the king of Babylon from 538 until 515 B.C. unless Cyrus is to be identified as the current king of Babylon. Second, Daniel obviously anticipates in 9:2 that the end of the seventy years is about to take place. That is why he prays to the Lord and asks Him to restore His people. Daniel was taken captive in 605 B.C. and realizes that he has now been in Babylon almost 70 years. Note that the words of Jeremiah are said to have originated with Yahweh, a strong assertion for inspiration (cf. 2 Pet. 1:20-21).

Another possible fulfillment of the words of Jeremiah is Jeremiah 51:1, 11. In these verses, the Lord announces the destruction of Babylon. This view is based on the close relationship between the phrases "the Lord stirred up the spirit of Cyrus king of Persia" in Ezra 1:1 and "the Lord has aroused the spirit of the kings of the Medes" in Jeremiah 51:11. Allen explains the logic of this view:

> The narrative provides its own clue [as to the fulfillment of Jeremiah's prophecy] in the phrase "the Lord stirred up the spirit." Jeremiah 51:1, 11 uses the same language in an oracle about the future destruction of Babylon. The latter verse is especially significant, with its statement that "The Lord has stirred up the spirit of the kings of the Medes." Cyrus, king of Anshan and Persia, became king of the

Medes by conquest in 549 B.C. before pressing on to capture Babylon in 539. This capture of Babylon made it possible for him to release the Judeans exiled to Babylonia, in the year 538. The narrator probably associated Jeremiah 51 with the even more relevant passages in Second Isaiah, which proclaim that Israel's God "stirred up" Cyrus in Isaiah 41:2, 25; 45:13. In these first two cases it was to conquer nations and in the last case to rebuild Jerusalem. In Isaiah 44:28, although the verb "stir up" is not used, the divine role given to Cyrus actually includes laying the temple foundations. There was therefore ample material to substantiate the narrative's appeal to prophetic prediction.[4]

A significant problem with this view is that the proclamation issued by Cyrus deals with the remnant's ability to return to their homeland. No mention is made of the destruction of Babylon, a noteworthy omission if this is the fulfillment that Ezra had in mind.

The Work of the Lord (1:1c)

The events of the book of Ezra are seen as having been arranged by divine decision. The text notes that the Lord "stirred up the spirit" of King Cyrus. Even though Cyrus is the most powerful man on the face of the earth, he is still just a pawn in God's hands, easily manipulated into fulfilling the desires of Yahweh. Other postexilic books also reference the work of God to "stir up the spirit" of men, even kings. 1 Chronicles 5:26 states that "the God of Israel stirred up the spirit of Pul, king of Assyria, even the spirit of Tilgathpilneser king of Assyria, and he carried them away into exile." Haggai writes that "the Lord stirred up the spirit of Zerubbabel the son of Shealtiel, governor of Judah, and the spirit of Joshua the son of Jehozadak, the high priest, and the spirit of all the remnant of the people" (Hag. 1:14)

This phrase reveals one of the major themes of the postexilic historical books, that is, the sovereignty of God. Ezra later records the work of the Lord to put it into the heart of Artaxerxes to allow Ezra to return to the Promised Land (7:27). He further writes that the Lord had "turned the heart of the king of Assyria [Darius] toward them [the Jewish remnant] to encourage them in the work of the house of God, the God of Israel" (6:22). Nehemiah consistently gives God the credit for his success (cf. Neh. 2:20; 6:16), even seeing Him as responsible for causing Artaxerxes to allow Nehemiah to return to Judah (cf. Neh. 2:4, 8). The very fact that both Ezra and Nehemiah consistently pray to the Lord demonstrates their belief in His sovereignty. Even though the name of God is not mentioned in the book of Esther, the major theme of the entire narrative is the sovereign providence of God. Like a puppet master pulling the strings of his marionettes, it is the Lord who orchestrates the succession of events that begin with the demotion of Vashti and promotion of Esther and result in the salvation of the Jews during the time of Xerxes. In each of these books, God is seen as completely sovereign, even over Cyrus, Darius, Xerxes, and Artaxerxes, the kings of the most powerful empire on earth.

The Proclamation Sent Throughout the kingdom (1:1d)

The text notes that the proclamation of Cyrus was put in writing. Throughout the postexilic historical books, there is a strong emphasis on the fact that the Persian kings wrote their decrees (cf. Ezra 6:2; Esth. 3:12; 8:9). The edicts of the Persian kings were written down and recorded because they were seen as irrevocable (Esth. 1:19; 8:8; Dan. 6:15). This decree was likely written in the Book of the Chronicles of the Kings of Media and Persia (cf. Esth. 10:2). The fact that this decree was written down allowed Darius to confirm its authenticity in chapter six. Of interest is the fact that this proclamation is the only official document in Ezra not written in Aramaic.

This proclamation issued by the king was sent throughout the entire kingdom of Persia. It is likely that several copies of the official proclamation would have been produced. These written proclamations may have taken the form of scrolls (cf. 6:2). These scrolls would have been sent to the various satraps who were then responsible to inform their constituents of the king's commands. Daniel reveals that the kingdom of Persia was made up of 120 satrapies soon after Cyrus took Babylon (Dan. 6:1). The postal system of the Persians was world-renowned. Herodotus, who traveled in Western Persia shortly after the reign of Xerxes, writes

Nothing mortal travels so fast as these Persian messengers. The entire plan is a Persian invention; and this is the method of it. Along the whole line of road there are men (they say) stationed with horses, in number equal to the number of days which the journey takes, allowing a man and horse to each day; and these men will not be hindered from accomplishing at their best speed the distance which they have to go, either by snow or rain, or heat, or by the darkness of night. The first rider delivers his dispatch to the second, and the second passes it to the third; and so it is borne from hand to hand along the whole line, like the light in the torch-race, which the Greeks celebrate to Vulcan. The Persians give the riding post in this manner, the name of "Angarum" (*Histories* 8.98).

It has been speculated that there must have been a supply station every twenty miles of so for this postal system to be most effective. The famed pony express (1860-61) covered over 1800 miles in a minimum of ten days, maintaining posts seven to twenty miles apart.[5]

Study Questions
1. Which prophet predicted the rise of Cyrus by name?
2. What was the name given to the collective group of Persian kings who reign during the events of the book of Ezra?
3. Which prophet predicted that Israel would serve Babylon seventy years?
4. Which of the two alternatives for the reckoning of Jeremiah's seventy years do you prefer? Why?
5. In what ways is the sovereignty of God demonstrated in the first verse of Ezra?
6. In what ways has the sovereignty of God been demonstrated in your own life?

Chapter 3
The Decree of Cyrus
Ezra 1:2-4

―――――∞∞∞―――――

Preview:

The decree of Cyrus allows the Jews to return to their homeland. The opportunity to live in the Promised Land which had been taken away by the Babylonians was now restored by the Persians. Furthermore, the decree allows the Jews to rebuild their temple, the centerpiece of their worship of Yahweh.

The Authority of Cyrus (1:2)

C yrus' decree begins with the standard Persian formula "Thus says Cyrus king of Persia." This was the customary way the Persians introduced edicts in both secular and religious contexts.[1] The introductory formula is followed by a declaration that Yahweh, God of heaven, had given Cyrus all the kingdoms of the earth. Cyrus indeed was able to conquer the known world during his reign. Cyrus recognizes that he was able to accomplish this feat with the aid of the gods. As a result, he pays homage to the God of the Jews. It is at once obvious that Cyrus made use of Jewish scribes as he writes his decree. The phrase "God of heaven" in reference to Yahweh, rarely used prior to the exile, becomes popular among the Jews during and after the exile (cf. Ezra 5:11, 12; 6:9, 10; 7:12, 21, 23; Neh. 1:4, 5; 2:4, 20; Dan. 2:18, 19, 37, 44).

At first glance this verse would seem to suggest that Cyrus believed in Yahweh, the God of the Jews. However, Cyrus allowed all foreigners who had been taken captive by the Babylonians to return to their homelands and rebuild their temples. Isaiah 45:4-5 indicates that Cyrus would be used by the Lord even though he did not truly "know" God. If Cyrus truly "knew" God he would not have acknowledged other gods (cf. Isa. 45:5). The truth of the matter is that Cyrus believed in and worshipped many different gods. The Cyrus Cylinder vividly testifies to this fact:

> I am Cyrus, king of the world, great king, mighty king, king of Babylon, king of the land of Sumer and Akkad, king of the four quarters, son of Cambyses, great king . . . progeny of an unending royal line, whose rule Bel and Nabu cherish, whose kingship they desire for their hearts' pleasures.

> When I, well-disposed, entered Babylon, I established the seat of government in the royal palace amidst jubilation and rejoicing. Marduk, the great god, caused the big-hearted inhabitants of Babylon to [illegible] me. I sought daily to worship him. . . .

> At my deeds Marduk, the great lord, rejoiced, and to me, Cyrus, the king who worshipped, and to Cambyses, my son, the offspring of my loins, and to all my troops, he graciously gave his blessing, and in good spirit . . . we glorified exceedingly his high divinity. . . .

May all the gods whom I have placed within their
sanctuaries address a daily prayer in my favor before
Bel and Nabu, that my days may long, and may they
say to Marduk my lord, may Cyrus the king who
reveres thee, and Cambyses his son . . . [illegible]
Obviously, the words of this cylinder reveal that Cyrus
was not a true believer in Yahweh. Cyrus makes the declaration that Marduk, not Yahweh, was responsible for his
successful campaign against the Babylonians. Marduk,
a storm god, was the patron god of Babylon and head of
the Mesopotamian pantheon of gods. The Mesopotamians
regarded Marduk as the supreme god and absolute ruler of
the universe. Cyrus claims to worship and revere Marduk,
even calling him the "great god." Cyrus also claims to be
king under the authority of Bel (another name for Marduk)
and Nabu, even commanding other gods to offer prayers
to these gods on his behalf. Nabu, the Babylonian god of
writing, is the son of Marduk. Bel and Nabu are pictured as
being carried into captivity in Isaiah 46:1, "Bel has bowed
down, Nebo [Nabu] stoops over; their images are consigned
to the beasts and the cattle. The things that you carry are
burdensome, A load for the weary beast."

Even though Cyrus does not truly believe that Yahweh
alone was responsible for his success, his words are true
nevertheless. The Lord had indeed given him all the kingdoms of the earth. Isaiah 45:1 informs us that the Lord had
raised up Cyrus to "subdue nations" and "loose the loins of
kings." Josephus records that Cyrus was shown the passages
from Isaiah which spoke of him and that "an earnest desire
and ambition seized upon him to fulfill what was so written"
(*Antiquities of the Jews* 11.1.2).

The Permission to Return to the Land (1:3)
This verse authorizes all ("whoever") the Jews living in
exile to return to the land of Judah and rebuild the temple of

Yahweh. Cyrus tells the captive Jews to "go up to Jerusalem," the central city of Judah. The phrase "go up to Jerusalem" is commonly used throughout the Old Testament to denote a trip to the City of David (e.g., 2 Sam. 19:34; 1 Kin. 12:27; 2 Kin. 12:17; Zech. 14:17). Because Jerusalem is situated on top of a mountain, travelers must literally ascend ("go up") to the city. The phrase "may his God be with him" was a customary way of wishing someone a safe journey, similar to our term "Godspeed."

From Cyrus' perspective, this return was probably optional, that is, the Jews were not required or forced to return to Jerusalem. However, from God's perspective, the return to the land seems to have been obligatory. Both Isaiah and Jeremiah call upon the nation to return following the exile (e.g., Isa. 48:20; Jer. 31:16-21). The author of the book of Chronicles also seems to call on the remnant to return after the exile. It is quite surprising that the Chronicler abbreviates the decree of Cyrus in 2 Chronicles 36:23 (cf. Ezra 1:2-4). This author believes that the major purpose in appending Cyrus' decree to the end of Chronicles was to provide a hopeful conclusion to the book. The decree is intentionally abbreviated to encourage the exiles to return to the land. Therefore, the final words an Israelite would read in the book of Chronicles ("and let him go up [to Jerusalem]") would be an exhortation to return to the land.

The city of Jerusalem ("city of peace") is located fourteen miles west of the Dead Sea and thirty-three miles east of the Mediterranean Sea. The city is situated on a rocky plateau 2,550 feet above sea level. It was centrally located in Israel and made an ideal capital. Jerusalem became the political capital of Israel early in the reign of King David (1011-971 B.C.).[2] It shortly became the religious capital of the nation as well with the building of the majestic Solomonic temple in 966 B.C. From this point forward, the city of Jerusalem occupied a place of prominence in the political and religious life of the nation. The city of Jerusalem occupies a central role in Ezra's narrative as it is the city in which the temple was to be built. The city is mentioned by name 48 times in the book of Ezra, at least once in every chapter.

The decree of Cyrus reveals the somewhat lenient attitude of the Persians regarding foreigners. In this regard, the foreign policy of the Persians was drastically different from that of the Assyrians and Babylonians, whose foreign policy involved the exile of vanquished nations and the transplantation of foreigners into the conquered territories. The foreign policy of the Persians was exactly the opposite; it allowed captive nations to return to their homelands. Cyrus hoped that his benevolence would lessen the chances of revolutions taking place throughout his vast empire. Happy citizens rarely rebel against the governing authorities. As Fensham explains, "it was a realistic policy that would create the maximum amount of contentment among the peoples under the jurisdiction of the Persians."[3] This policy of toleration on the part of Cyrus is well attested in ancient literature, including various portions of the Cyrus Cylinder. Note the following excerpts:

> My numerous troops moved about undisturbed in the midst of Babylon. I did not allow any to terrorize the land of Sumer and Akkad. I kept in view the needs of Babylon and all its sanctuaries to promote their well being. The citizens of Babylon . . . I lifted their unbecoming yoke. Their dilapidated dwellings I restored. I put an end to their misfortunes. . . . The holy cities beyond the Tigris whose sanctuaries had been in ruins over a long period, the gods whose abode is in the midst of them, I returned to the places and housed them in lasting abodes. I gathered together all their inhabitants and restored to them their dwellings. The gods of Sumer and Akkad whom Nabonidus [Babylonian king] had, to the anger of

the lord of the gods, brought into Babylon, I at the bidding of Marduk, the great lord, made to dwell in peace in their habitations, delightful abodes.

Yamauchi adds, "especially impressive corroborative evidence of Cyrus's policy of toleration are the 'Verse Account of Nabonidus' and the 'Cyrus Cylinder,' which indicate that one of the first acts of Cyrus was to return the gods which had been removed from their sanctuaries by Nabonidus."[4]

Another major reason why the foreign policy of the Persians was so lenient was due to their religious beliefs. The Persians of the Achaemenid period followed a religion founded by Zoroaster.[5] Zoroaster preached an ethical dualism, with two primordial uncreated Spirits, a Good Spirit (Ahura Mazda) and an Evil Spirit (Angra Mainyu). It is the responsibility of each person to choose which Spirit to follow. Because the Persians believed in this simplistic dualism instead of a powerful cultic god (e.g., Baal, Dagon, Marduk), they were quite tolerant of other religions. Blenkinsopp explains, "In the absence of an imperial cult of the type of the Assyrian Ashur, the Achaemenids tolerated and even cultivated local deities as imperial patrons."[6] It has even been stated that "it was Persian policy to support religion."[7] Instead of the local cultic worship promoting insubordination as the Assyrians and Babylonians believed, it was viewed by the Persians as a soothing practice. Blenkinsopp writes, "the temple may . . . have been seen as a point of convergence for the symbolic structures of the region, an 'emblem of collective identity,' thereby mitigating to some extent the inevitable resentment generated by subjection to a foreign power."[8] This generous religious policy dramatically affected the Jewish remnant as it allowed them to rebuild their temple and reinstitute Yahweh worship in the land of Israel.

This is not to say, however, that the Persians were lenient in all their policies. Their system of taxation, for example, placed a considerable burden on the returned remnant. Blenkinsopp explains,

> The imperial policy of the Achaemenids [Persian dynasty of kings] is often taken to be more benign that [sic] that of their predecessors. They appear to have been well disposed toward their Jewish subjects, but their fiscal policy was every bit as harsh and unenlightened as that of the Assyrians and Babylonians. The point has been made that taxation was a severe burden which increased with the passage of time and contributed substantially to unrest and rebellion. The tendency to hoard bullion also left the provinces with inadequate resources for maintaining a flourishing or even viable economy. The practice of farming out the collection of taxes to large businesses (e.g., the Murashu house in Nippur and the Egibi in Babylon) or prominent members of local aristocracies was another factor creating disaffection and division.[9]

This heavy burden of taxation plays a key role in Nehemiah's narrative as we see some of the returned remnant forced into slavery as a result of the oppressive conditions (Neh. 5:5).

Cyrus revealed in 1:2 that the Lord appointed him to build a house in Jerusalem. Here, he authorizes the Jews to rebuild that house, namely, the "house of the Lord, the God of Israel." The phrase "house of the Lord" is a reference to the temple built for Yahweh by Solomon in 966 B.C. This temple had been burned by the armies of Nebuchadnezzar when they destroyed the city of Jerusalem in 586 B.C. (cf. 2 Kin. 25:9; 2 Chr. 36:19). The edict given here is in perfect keeping with Cyrus' religious beliefs. As noted earlier, according to Cyrus, since the gods had given him success in battle, he was responsible to honor them by rebuilding their temples and having sacrifices offered in their names. The phrase "He is the God who is in Jerusalem" is further indication of the fact that Cyrus did not truly worship God.

The Call for Support (1:4)

The final portion of Cyrus' decree concerns the support necessary to carry out this decree. The reference to "every survivor" is surely a reference to the Jews who had survived the captivity. Unfortunately, many Jews had not survived the captivity. The reference to the "men of that place" is clearly referring to the neighbors of the Jews who are returning to Jerusalem. What is not so clear, however, is the national heritage of these neighbors. One view is that the phrase is a general reference to the Gentile neighbors of the returning Jews. This view is held by Allen who envisions this return as a second Exodus.[10] Accordingly, he sees the assistance provided to the returning exiles by their Gentile neighbors as parallel to the contributions presented to the generation of Moses by the Egyptians (Ex. 12:35-36).

A second view is that the phrase refers to those Jews who remained in exile. This view is held by Fensham who writes, "It would have been indeed a strange situation if non-Jewish inhabitants of the Persian Empire were called on to assist the Jews."[11] This latter view seems best. Those Jews who remained in a position of prosperity were asked to help support those who ventured home. Many Jews were reluctant to leave their new homes. Josephus records that many Jews decided not to return because they did not want to leave their possessions (*Antiquities of the Jews*, 11.1.3). Williamson correctly observes, "Not all Jews by any means wanted to return. They were therefore encouraged to assist those who did. At no point is a reference to their Gentile neighbors either necessary or historically credible."[12] Since Cyrus made a series of decrees allowing all captive peoples to return to their homelands, it would have placed an incredible strain on the inhabitants of Babylon if they had to support every group that chose to return. The fact that these neighbors also contributed a "freewill offering for the house of God" further indicates that these were individuals who worshipped that God, namely, the Jews.

The Jewish remnant that remained in Babylon supported their brethren with monetary wealth ("silver and gold") as well as material goods and cattle. They also contributed a "freewill offering" (Hebrew *nedabah*) to be taken to the temple. The exact nature of this offering is unknown. It is doubtful that the reference is to money since silver and gold has already been mentioned. It is also unlikely that the reference is to meal or grain offerings since these might have spoiled or rotted prior to the time of sacrifice. The offering probably consisted of a herd of animals to be sacrificed on the rebuilt altar. In 3:5, the same word is used to denote the freewill offerings of the remnant which were burnt on the altar.

Study Questions
1. Who gave Cyrus "all the kingdoms of the earth?"
2. Do you believe that Cyrus will be in heaven? Why or why not?
3. Who is Marduk?
4. What does the phrase "go up to Jerusalem" mean?
5. Which prophets call upon the nation to return following the exile?
6. Why does the Chronicler abbreviate the decree of Cyrus?
7. How many times is the city of Jerusalem mentioned in the book of Ezra?
8. Why was the foreign policy of the Persians so lenient?
9. Why would some Jews choose to remain in Babylon rather than return to the Promised Land?

Chapter 4
The Support for the People
Ezra 1:5-11

—⚬⚬⚬—

Preview:
   The Jews who chose not to return to Jerusalem offer to help those who did choose to return. Cyrus himself provides considerable support, including the return of the articles of Yahweh which had been taken to Babylon by Nebuchadnezzar. Was the Ark of the Covenant among these articles? Read on to find the answer.

The Support of the Neighbors (1:5-6)

Just as the Lord had "stirred up" the spirit of Cyrus in 1:1, here He "stirred up" the spirit of the exiles. Judah and Benjamin are the only tribes mentioned by name in verse five, most likely because these were the primary tribes taken to Babylon when Nebuchadnezzar destroyed Jerusalem. The tribe of Levi is also referenced through the mention of the priests and Levites. Certainly many priests and Levites would have remained in the Southern Kingdom when the Northern Kingdom fell since it was their responsibility to care for the temple in Jerusalem. In fact, the majority of priests and Levites already lived in the Southern Kingdom, having been expelled from the Northern Kingdom by Jeroboam (cf. 2 Chr. 11:14). Many other families from the other tribes likewise lived in the Southern Kingdom (cf. 2 Chr. 11:16-17). 2 Chronicles 30:11 identifies men from the tribes of Asher, Manasseh, and Zebulun as among those who apparently moved to Jerusalem following the call of Hezekiah while verse18 of the same chapter adds Ephraim and Issachar. The descendants of these men would have been taken to Babylon along with the tribes of Judah and Benjamin. There are no so-called lost tribes of Israel (cf. Rev. 7:4).

The support mentioned in these verses refers back to verse four where Cyrus calls on the "men of that place" to support the Jews who are journeying to Jerusalem. This support likely came from Jewish neighbors rather than from the Gentiles. Although these Jews did not choose to return themselves, they did offer aid to those who did return. This aid took the form of silver, gold, goods, cattle, and valuables and was in addition to the gifts provided as a freewill offering.

The Support of Cyrus (1:7-11)

In accordance with his attempt to gain the favor of Yahweh, Cyrus returns the articles which had been taken from the house of the Lord in Jerusalem. These articles had been taken by Nebuchadnezzar during his campaigns against Judah in 605, 597, and 586 B.C. These articles had been treated as trophies and otherwise misused by the Babylonian kings (cf. Dan. 5:1-4). They were also placed "in the house of his gods," a reference to the various temples of the gods worshipped by Nebuchadnezzar. This was common practice in the Ancient Near East. The Philistines, after defeating the

Israelites at Ebenezer and capturing the Ark of the Covenant, took the golden Ark to the city of Ashdod and placed it in the temple of Dagon (1 Sam. 5:1-2). The Moabite Stone records the victory of Mesha over an Israelite town, at which point he "took from there the vessels of Yahweh and dragged them before Chemosh" (lines 17-18), a reference to the temple of the Moabite god. Ordinarily, the idols of foreign nations would have been placed in these temples. However, since the Jews had no graven images of their God, the vessels used in the cultic worship of the Jews were taken to Babylon. Interestingly enough, the same Hebrew word (*yatza'*) is used to describe the actions of both Cyrus ("brought out") and Nebuchadnezzar ("carried away"). The significance of the repeated term is that it shows that Cyrus was righting the wrong that Nebuchadnezzar had done.

Cyrus ordered his royal treasurer Mithredath to distribute the temple articles to Sheshbazzar, the "prince" of the Jews. Evidently, when the Persians took Babylon they immediately placed these valuable articles into their treasury. Mithredath was a common Persian name meaning "given to Mithra." Mithra was the Persian sun god, one of the most ancient of all Persian gods.

Sheshbazzar is a Babylonian name meaning "Shamash protects the son." Shamash was the Babylonian sun god. Sheshbazzar is identified simply by name, without even a patronym. If Sheshbazzar is identified as the Shenazzar of 1 Chronicles 3:18, then Sheshbazzar was the uncle of Zerubbabel (cf. 1 Chr. 3:19) and would probably have been about 60 years old at the time of the return. Some have advanced the theory that Sheshbazzar and Zerubbabel were the same person, Sheshbazzar being Zerubbabel's Aramaic name (e.g., Josephus, *Antiquities of the Jews* 11.13.92). It was common for the Jews in exile to have two names (e.g. Daniel and Belteshazzar; Hadassah and Esther). However, it is clear from Ezra 5:14-16 and 1 Esdras 6:18 that Sheshbazzar and Zerubbabel were not one and the same.

Sheshbazzar was the original leader of the Jews who decided to return to Judah. The Hebrew word translated "prince" (*nasi'*) simply means "leader" or "chief." It does not have the inherent meaning of "son of a king" as the English usage might imply. However, if Sheshbazzar is to be identified as Shenazzar, then he would indeed be a prince since his father would have been Jeconiah (Jehoiachin). This would also make him the uncle of Zerubbabel. If Zerubbabel was the nephew of Sheshbazzar, it would help explain why and how he became the governor of Judah (cf. Hag. 1:1). It would also reveal the fact that the Persians attempted to utilize the House of David in their governmental system. Sheshbazzar is mentioned only in the book of Ezra (1:8, 11; 5:14, 16). Sheshbazzar was appointed by Cyrus to be the governor of Judah when the initial returnees reached Jerusalem. How long he held this position is unclear. What is clear is that Zerubbabel has succeeded Sheshbazzar as the governor of Judah by 520 B.C. (cf. Hag. 1:1).

The figures of verses nine through eleven do not add up. The total number of the articles identified in verses nine and ten is 2,499. Verse eleven reveals that the total number of articles returned to Jerusalem was 5,400. It is possible that verses nine and ten include only the largest, most important vessels while verse eleven records the total of all the vessels, including the less significant ones. It is also possible that the articles enumerated in verses nine and ten were those taken by Nebuchadnezzar and returned by Cyrus while the total number in verse eleven includes the articles donated by the neighbors of the Jews (cf. 1:4, 6). The translation "duplicates" in verse nine is better rendered "utensils" (NET) or "knives" (NKJV).

Verse eleven identifies the exiles who returned with Sheshbazzar as having originated in Babylon. The city of

Babylon (Akkadian *babilu*, meaning "gate of god") is one of the oldest cities of civilization. The city was founded by Nimrod, the son of Cush (Gen. 10:8-10). It later became the site of the Tower of Babel. Babylon is located on the Euphrates River almost 200 miles north of the Persian Gulf. The Euphrates River ran right through the middle of the city, effectively dividing the city into two halves, the eastern and the western. The city began its rise to prominence in approximately 1830 B.C. The most significant ruler of this early period was Hammurabi (ca. 1728-1686 B.C.). The city achieved the height of its glory during the reign of Nebuchadnezzar (605-562 B.C.). This is also the period of the Jewish exile in Babylon. Nebuchadnezzar beautified the city by constructing a series of magnificent gardens, a creation which quickly became known as one of the seven wonders of the ancient world. He also built the Ishtar Gate and restored the Temple of Marduk. Herodotus reports that the city was in the form of a square, measuring 120 stade (13 miles) on each side (*Histories* 1.178-86).

The phrase "from Babylon to Jerusalem" marks a dramatic turning point in Israel's history. The history of God's people can be recounted in geographical terms. Abraham journeyed to the land God showed him. The family of Jacob moved to Egypt. The generations of Moses and Joshua left Egypt and journeyed to the Promised Land. The generations of Hoshea and Zedekiah were exiled throughout Assyria and Babylon. Each of these movements marked a significant turning point for the children of Israel. This passage is no less important. It reveals that God was still providentially watching over His people and determining their fate. In fact, the verb translated "went up" is in the passive tense, thus denoting divine activity (cf. "the exiles were brought up," NRSV). God is the one who is bringing the exiles back to the land. Even in the midst of their march into exile, God promised the Jews that He would bring them back to the land which had been promised to them (Jer. 31:15-17). This phrase marks the initial fulfillment of that promise.

Throughout this opening chapter the author reveals the relationship between the generation who returned and their ancestors. He explicitly states that the return fulfilled prophecy, he claims that it was Yahweh who moved the heart of Cyrus to issue his proclamation, he identifies the returnees as members of the tribes of Judah, Benjamin, and Levi, and he records the inventory of temple articles that were returned to the temple in Jerusalem. Each of these indicate that this current generation still stood in a covenantal relationship with their God and would still receive the blessings promised to their ancestors if they were obedient. This reality is the major theme of the book of Ezra.

While the general stipulations of the covenants were unconditional, the time at which the nation would receive their blessings was conditional upon repentance. It should be noted that within the promises themselves was the assumption that the people would be disobedient and receive the ultimate curse promised in Deuteronomy 28, that is, the loss of their promised land and an exile to a foreign land (cf. Deut. 30:1-5). The nation's disobedience, however, would not nullify the promises made to their ancestors; promises which are still in effect today (Rom. 11:28-29).

It should not be assumed that the promises given to the patriarchs were completely fulfilled with this initial return to the land on the part of Sheshbazzar and his followers. While similarities do exist, the fact remains that the events prophesied in Deuteronomy 30:1-10 have not been fulfilled even unto the modern day. Deuteronomy 30:1-10 makes several promises which have never been fulfilled. First, the Jews have never been completely regathered to the land (4). Second, the Jews have never truly "possessed" the land (5). Third, the Jews have never prospered as they did under the reigns of David and Solomon (5, 9). And fourth, the Jews have never had their hearts "circumcised" to be able to love the Lord their God with all their heart and with all their soul (6). These promises still await a future day (i.e., the Millennial Kingdom). These promises are conditional upon the nation's repentance, when they will finally say "blessed is He who comes in the name of the Lord" (cf. Matt. 23:39).

Where is the Ark of the Covenant?

There is no mention here of the Ark of the Covenant or of the other major articles of furniture originally placed in the temple. The Ark of the Covenant was the most significant piece of furniture in the temple. It was crafted by Bezalel and Oholiab out of acacia wood overlaid with gold (cf. Ex. 25:10-11; 31:1-11). The Ark of the Covenant contained a golden pot full of manna, Aaron's rod that budded, and the tablets of the covenant (Heb. 9:4). It resided in the Holy of Holies in the tabernacle and, subsequently, the temple (Heb. 9:3-4). 2 Chronicles 36:18 suggests that all of the major articles of furniture were taken to Babylon by Nebuchadnezzar. The question is whether or not the Ark of the Covenant was still in the city of Jerusalem when Nebuchadnezzar took the city in 586 B.C.

There are four major views concerning the location of the Ark of the Covenant. The first view asserts that the ark was removed from the temple during the reign of Solomon by Menelik I and taken to Aksum in Ethiopia. According to tradition, Menelik I was the son of Solomon and the Queen of Sheba. The second view alleges that the ark was removed from the temple during the reign of Rehoboam by Pharaoh Shishak of Egypt. In 926 B.C., Shishak "came up against Jerusalem and he took away the treasures of the house of the Lord and the treasures of the king's house, and he took everything, even taking all the shields of gold which Solomon had made" (1 Kin. 14:25-26). This view is the basis for the movie "Raiders of the Lost Ark."

These first two views seem to be disproved by 2 Chronicles 35:3, "He [Josiah] also said to the Levites who taught all Israel and who were holy to the Lord, 'Put the holy ark in the house which Solomon the son of David king of Israel built; it will be a burden on your shoulders no longer. Now serve the Lord your God and His people Israel.'" Josiah gives this command in his eighteenth year (cf. 2 Chr. 35:19; 622-621 B.C.), hundreds of years after the reigns of Solomon and Rehoboam. In fact, the Ark of the Covenant still seems to be in Jerusalem as late as 591 B.C. In 591 B.C., the sixth year of King Jehoiachin's exile (cf. Ezek. 1:2; 8:1), Ezekiel sees the Shekinah glory of the Lord leave the temple and stop above the Mount of Olives (cf. Ezek. 10:18; 11:23). Since the Shekinah glory of the Lord resided above the wings of the cherubim on the Ark of the Covenant, it is logical to assume that the ark is still in the temple at this point.

The third view holds that the ark was removed from the temple by the prophet Jeremiah at some point just prior to the city's destruction by Nebuchadnezzar in 586 B.C. This tradition is based on the apocryphal account of 2 Maccabees 2:4-5, "It was also contained in the same writing, that the prophet, being warned of God, commanded the tabernacle and the ark to go with him, as he went forth into the mountain, where Moses climbed up, and saw the heritage of God. And when Jeremiah came thither, he found a hollow cave, wherein he laid the tabernacle, and the ark, and the altar of incense, and so stopped the door." The primary difficulty with this view is that Jeremiah was viewed as a traitor by the religious leaders of his day. In fact, on one occasion Pashhur, the chief officer of the temple, had Jeremiah beaten and put in stocks (Jer. 20:1-2). On another occasion, the priests seized him and called for his execution (Jer. 26:8). When Jeremiah finally did try to leave Jerusalem, he was arrested and accused of being a traitor (Jer. 37:12-16). In light of these passages, it is hard to believe that he could have entered the temple and taken its greatest treasures.

The fourth view maintains that the ark was taken to Babylon by Nebuchadnezzar when he took the city of Jerusalem in 586 B.C. 2 Chronicles 36:18 states, "And all the articles of the house of God, great and small, and the treasures of the house of the Lord, and the treasures of the king and of his officers, he [Nebuchadnezzar] brought them all to Babylon." One must assume that if the Ark of the Covenant was in the temple at this point, and there is little reason to believe that it wasn't, then it must have been taken to Babylon by Nebuchadnezzar. Since Ezra makes no mention of its return, it can be assumed that it had been destroyed in Babylon, perhaps even melted down to help create the statue of gold described in Daniel three. Josephus makes no mention of the Ark of the Covenant in his description of Herod's temple, "But the inmost part of the temple of all was twenty cubits. This was also separated from the outer part by a veil. In this there was nothing at all. It was inaccessible and inviolable, and not to be seen by any; and was called the Holy of Holies" (*Wars of the Jews* 5.5.5). The Ark of the Covenant is likewise absent from Ezekiel's vision of the millennial temple (Ezek. 40-48).

Study Questions
1. What three tribes are referenced in verse five?
2. Who is the "prince of Judah" in this passage?
3. Who founded the city of Babylon?
4. What was kept in the Ark of the Covenant?
5. What resided above the wings of the cherubim on the Ark of the Covenant?
6. What do you think happened to the Ark of the Covenant?

Chapter 5
The Introduction to the List of Returnees
Ezra 2:1-2a

—⁂—

Preview:
   This passage introduces us to two of the great leaders in the book of Ezra, Zerubbabel and Jeshua. Zerubbabel, the political leader, and Jeshua, the religious leader, work hand in hand to lead the restoration of the Jews. So significant is their partnership that the prophet Zechariah uses it to describe the coming Messiah, Jesus Christ.

T hese introductory verses explain the contents of the rest of the chapter. What follows is a list of those Jews who returned to Jerusalem from Babylon. The section is set apart from the narrative by means of an inclusio (note the use of the word "city" in verses one and seventy). An inclusio occurs when similar or identical phrases, motifs, or episodes begin and end a literary unit. While the inclusion of this list may cause many modern readers to skip this chapter of scripture, its significance for the original readers cannot be overstated. These were the great heroes of the past, those who had taken the first step towards rebuilding the nation of Israel. Many of the original readers in Judah could directly trace their roots back to those who returned to the land a hundred years earlier.

One Return or Two?

The list of chapter two clearly goes with the events of chapter three where Jeshua and Zerubbabel offer sacrifices to the Lord upon their return. What is not so clear, however, is the relationship between chapters one and two. Since Sheshbazzar is not mentioned in chapter two many have supposed that the text is describing two different returns. Those who hold to two returns have speculated that there might be a significant time gap between the return of chapter one under the leadership of Sheshbazzar and the return of chapter two, seemingly under Zerubbabel and Jeshua.[1] Haggai makes it clear that Zerubbabel and Jeshua are in Jerusalem by the second year of Darius (i.e., 520 B.C.). Hence, Sheshbazzar's return occurred in 538 B.C. and Zerubbabel's return occurred sometime between 538 and 520 B.C.

While two returns are possible, it seems best to identify the return of Zerubbabel with that of Sheshbazzar. One can't help but expect that the narrative would have noted the date of the second return if there were two separate returns. Ezra routinely supplies the date of the significant events that he records (cf. 1:1; 3:8; 7:7). Also, the reference to the seventh month in 3:1 is without context if the year is not the first year of Cyrus (cf. 1:1). Since 3:8 refers to the "second year of their coming," it can be assumed that the first year of their coming was also the first year of Cyrus.

The Purpose of the List

The purpose of this list in the narrative of Ezra is also heavily debated. It is possible that the list was included to reveal which inhabitants of Judah were true Israelites as opposed to the Samaritans. One noteworthy problem with this view is that many of the individuals in the list are identified by place rather than lineage. Another problem with this view is that there are many foreign names included on the list. A second possibility is that the list served as a tax record for the Persians. The major difficulty with this view is that a tax record would likely include all inhabitants of a city, not just the Jews. A final possibility is that the list was included to restore land rights. When the Babylonians took the Jews into exile they confiscated much of the property of Judah. Inclusion in the list would thus serve as a sort of deed or title to one's property. This view helps to explain the many geographical references included in the list. The inclusion of the list also serves to show the continuation between the preexilic community and the postexilic community, a major theme of Ezra. Nehemiah utilizes this list to serve his own purposes, that is, to emphasize the faithfulness of the previous generations in an effort to repopulate the city of Jerusalem.

The list of Nehemiah 7 contains several differences from the list of Ezra 2. Allrik provides a table listing twenty-nine differences between the lists of Nehemiah 7 and Ezra 2 out of the 153 individual numerals or ciphers. The divergences usually occur in proper names and in numerical statistics. He believes the discrepancies between the lists to be the result of scribal error.[2] One does not have to come to the conclusion that Nehemiah used Ezra's list when he composed his work. It is quite possible that Ezra and Nehemiah utilized two different lists for their respective accounts. One would assume that there was more than one list of the original returnees. And certainly both authors would have had access to the official records of their province. For Nehemiah's part, he informs us that he took his list from "the book of the genealogy of those who came up first" (Neh. 7:5). This hardly seems to be a reference to the book of Ezra. Ezra does not tell us where he found his list. It is unlikely that he copied his list from the book of Nehemiah since he probably wrote before Nehemiah.

The Contents of the List (2:1)
This first verse reveals the contents of the list. The roster that follows is a record of those who returned to the region of Judah from Babylon subsequent to the decree of Cyrus. The province referred to in this verse is probably that of Judah rather than Babylonia, although either is possible. The ancestors of those who were returning had originally lived in Judah. They had been carried away into exile by Nebuchadnezzar, king of Babylon, in 586 B.C. As noted earlier, Nebuchadnezzar's foreign policy involved the exile of conquered peoples throughout the empire.

Cyrus is obviously attempting to right the wrongs of the Babylonians. The previous chapter explained how Cyrus returned to the Jews the temple articles which had been taken by Nebuchadnezzar. Here, the emphasis is on the return of the cities and homes of the Jews which Nebuchadnezzar had given to others. The phrase "each to his city" shows that the Jews were the rightful owners of the territory of Judah. The region had been divided up and given to individual families during the time of Joshua (Josh. 13-20). That is why the list that follows is divided according to genealogical lineage. Each family was expected to return to the property originally given to their ancestors.

The Leaders of the Return (2:2a)
The first half of verse two lists the major leaders who led the return to Jerusalem. There are eleven names listed

here. Nehemiah adds one more, that of Nahamani (Neh. 7:7). Nehemiah's list is probably original as the number twelve would be used to represent the twelve tribes of Israel. Zerubbabel and Jeshua are named first. These two individuals are clearly the major leaders in Ezra 1-6. They are routinely mentioned together (cf. 3:2, 8; 4:3; 5:2). With the exception of 3:2, Zerubbabel is always mentioned first. Zerubbabel served as the governor of Judah while Jeshua served as the high priest. Together they represented the political and religious leadership of the nation. They work together to return to the land (2:2), to lay the foundation of the temple (3:8-10), to respond to the enemies of Judah (4:1-3), and to resume the rebuilding of the temple (5:2). So significant is their partnership that the prophet Zechariah uses it to describe the coming "Branch" (Zech. 6:12). From Jeremiah 23:5 it is clear that the "Branch" is going to come from the line of David and will "reign as king." Zechariah uses Jeshua to illustrate that this "Branch" will also "build the temple of the Lord" and "be a priest on His throne" (Zech. 6:12-13). The "Branch" is an obvious prophetic reference to Jesus Christ who unites the offices of both King and Priest (cf. Psalm 110; Heb. 7).

The name Zerubbabel means "the seed of Babel" or "born in Babel." He is not to be identified with the Sheshbazzar of chapter one. Zerubbabel is one of the most popular figures in the Bible. He is mentioned in 1 Chronicles, Ezra, Nehemiah, Haggai, Zechariah, Matthew, and Luke. 1 Chronicles 3:17-19 informs us that Zerubbabel was the grandson of Jeconiah (Jehoiachin), one of the kings of Judah. There is some question as to the identity of Zerubbabel's father. 1 Chronicles 3:19 identifies Zerubbabel as the son of Pedaiah while Ezra names him as the son of Shealtiel (cf. 3:2). Since all other accounts identify Zerubbabel as the son of Shealtiel it is clear that Ezra is correct. This does not necessarily mean, however, that Chronicles is wrong. It is possible that this is a case of levirate marriage. If Shealtiel had died without an heir, then Pedaiah could have married his widow, thereby producing an heir through their union. The resultant child would take Shealtiel as his family name even though Pedaiah would have been his biological father (cf. Deut. 25:5-6). Another problem concerning Zerubbabel is the nature of his position in the rebuilding project. On several occasions Zerubbabel is given credit for the rebuilding of the temple (cf. Ezra 3:2; 5:2; Hag. 2:4; Zech. 4:9). However, in Ezra 5:16 Sheshbazzar is given credit for starting the rebuilding project. There are three proposed solutions to this problem while still keeping Zerubbabel and Sheshbazzar separate. First, it is possible that Sheshbazzar returned to Jerusalem prior to Zerubbabel and began the rebuilding project. Subsequently, Zerubbabel returned and completed the work. Second, it is possible that Sheshbazzar and Zerubbabel returned together. In this scenario, Sheshbazzar was the original leader of the Jews who led the return and started to rebuild the temple. He was succeeded by Zerubbabel when he left office, perhaps due to his death. Zerubbabel then finished the rebuilding of the temple. Third, it is possible that both returned together and that Sheshbazzar was the Persian official responsible for overseeing the work while Zerubbabel and the Jews actually rebuilt the temple. In the eyes of the Persians it was Sheshbazzar who rebuilt the temple while in the eyes of the Jews it was Zerubbabel who accomplished the feat. The second option seems best. It is clear from the prophecies of Haggai and Zechariah that the work of the temple had ceased for a number of years. The Lord used Haggai and Zechariah to rebuke the people and motivate them to finish the rebuilding effort. Since Sheshbazzar is never mentioned by these prophets it can be assumed that he was no longer in a position of leadership.

Zerubbabel's portrait in Ezra and Nehemiah is worthy of consideration. These books identify Zerubbabel simply as the son of Shealtiel. As noted earlier, Zerubbabel is the grandson of Jeconiah, a king of Judah. In addition, Haggai and Zechariah portray Zerubbabel as the heir of the Davidic dynasty. For these prophets, the presence of Zerubbabel is the sign or proof that the Davidic line is still unbroken (cf. Hag. 2, Zech. 4). It has also been noted earlier that Zerubbabel was the governor of Judah. Yet, Ezra and Nehemiah never identify Zerubbabel as the grandson of Jeconiah and heir to the throne or even as the governor of Judah. Clearly, this oversight is intentional and the question of Ezra and Nehemiah's silence concerning Zerubbabel's pedigree is unavoidable.

Why would these books intentionally conceal Zerubbabel's identity? The answer is to be found in the overall perception of Ezra and Nehemiah regarding the nation's political relationship to the Persian Empire. Ezra and Nehemiah both regard the Persians as the rulers of Judah. This political reality is understood as a form of God's providence for His people. It is clear from passages like Isaiah 45:1 that the Persians were God's instruments of salvation for His people. Throughout Ezra and Nehemiah the Persian kings are pictured as the mediating agents though which God accomplishes His purposes regarding the remnant. It is the Persian kings who allow the return to the land (Cyrus), the initial rebuilding of the temple (Cyrus), the subsequent continuation of the temple project after a hiatus (Darius), the establishment of worship (Cyrus), and the rebuilding of the walls of the city (Artaxerxes). Nowhere is found the aspirations of independence so common in other exilic and postexilic books (cf. Ezekiel, Daniel, Haggai, Zechariah). Ezra and Nehemiah are content to accept this situation and faithfully serve the Persians. Japhet believes that their acceptance of this situation was because they understood it "not only as an expression of God's will and sovereign guidance of the world, but as a divine grace and as God's way of redeeming His people."[3] As a result of this political reality, the theological theme of the House of David as the vehicle of redemption is intentionally ignored by Ezra and Nehemiah.

The name Jeshua means "salvation." It is the Old Testament equivalent of the name Jesus. Jeshua was the son of Jozadak. He was of the priestly family of Jedaiah, one of the 24 priestly families that David organized (cf. 1 Chr. 24:7). He was also the grandson of Seraiah, the high priest at the time of the destruction of Jerusalem (cf. 1 Chr. 6:14; 2 Kin. 25:18). Jeshua was the first high priest of the returned remnant. The office of high priest becomes much more prominent and powerful during the post-exilic period. This phenomenon continues through the time of Christ.

The Nehemiah named here is not to be identified with the Nehemiah who rebuilt the walls of the city in 444 B.C. This return takes place almost 100 years before Nehemiah's return. Nehemiah, meaning "the Lord comforts," was evidently a popular name in the exilic community (cf. Neh. 3:16). It is theoretically possible but highly improbable that the Seraiah referenced here is the father of Ezra. Also, the Mordecai mentioned here should not be mistaken with the Mordecai of the book of Esther. That Mordecai is still in the Persian capital of Susa some fifty years after this return.

Study Questions
1. What is an inclusion?
2. Do you believe Zerubbabel and Jeshua returned with Sheshbazzar? Why or why not?
3. Why do you think the list of chapter two is included in the narrative of Ezra?
4. Are the lists of Ezra 2 and Nehemiah 7 identical?
5. What is recorded in the list of chapter two?
6. Who is the "Branch?"
7. Why do the books of Ezra and Nehemiah intentionally conceal Zerubbabel's identity?
8. What does the name Jeshua mean?

Chapter 6
The Roster of Returnees
Ezra 2:2b-70

—————

Preview:

Many people in the United States can trace their lineage back to the pilgrims who took a leap of faith and came to America on the Mayflower. The reason they are able to do that is because we have a roster of those who originally sailed on the Mayflower. Many Jews in the original audience of Ezra could trace their lineage back to the original group that took a leap of faith and returned to the Promised Land. The reason they were able to do that is because of the list provided in this chapter.

The List of Those with Proof of Ancestry (2:2b-58)

Verses 2b-35 identify the family leaders who returned with Zerubbabel. The designations "sons of" (Hebrew *bene*) and "men of" (Hebrew *'aneshe*) in these verses indicate the two ways by which the exiles could validate their

Jewish ancestry, either by family name or by location in Judah. However, these designations are not always exact. For example, the word *bene* is used in verse one even though it clearly refers to a geographical location (i.e., province). It is also used in verse 21 with Bethlehem, clearly a reference to a city. Likewise in verse 34 with Jericho, again a reference to a city. It is unknown if the word *'aneshe* occurs with any family names in this list.

When one compares this list with that of Nehemiah 7 it is at once obvious that there are several scribal errors throughout. While the proper names are almost exact between the two lists the numerical notations frequently disagree. These disagreements seemingly occur at random. Neither list consistently has the higher number. Although scribes took great care to ensure the accuracy of their work, numerical lists invariably proved to be the most difficult of all passages to accurately reproduce.

Verses 36-39 identify the priests who returned. The priests were the descendants of Aaron, a subset of the Levites. While all priests were Levites, not all Levites were priests. These names represent only four of the 24 priestly families that David organized (cf. 1 Chr. 24:7-18). Although Passhur is not mentioned in 1 Chronicles 24 it is likely that he represents the line of Malchijah (cf. 1 Chr. 9:12; 24:9). The priests comprised roughly a tenth of the total returnees (4,289). These numbers were sufficient to serve the needs of the temple system. This seems to be the most carefully transmitted portion of the list (cf. Neh. 7:39-42). Special mention is made in verse 36 of the house of Jeshua, the first postexilic high priest.

Verses 40-42 identify the Levites who returned. Only 341 Levites chose to return with Zerubbabel (Nehemiah records 360; cf. Neh. 7:43-45). This is a small number in comparison to the number of priests who returned. This problem was still not resolved by the time of Ezra's return (c. 458 B.C.). For example, in 8:15-30 Ezra describes his problems in finding sufficient numbers of Levites. It is possible that many chose not to return because their work was not viewed as significant. The Levites were to serve as assistants to the sons of Aaron in the service of the Tabernacle (cf. Num. 18:4). They would have been responsible for cleaning the various pieces of furniture, baking the showbread, inspecting animals for sacrifices, and generally making sure that everything involved in the cultic process was done according to the Mosaic Law.

Within the larger group of Levites two guilds are identified; the temple singers and the gatekeepers. The temple singers were often associated with the Levites (cf. Neh. 11-12) and were primarily responsible for leading the music during worship. The gatekeepers were responsible for guarding the gates leading into the temple as well as locking and unlocking the doors of the temple. They also watched over the temple chambers and treasuries (1 Chr. 9:17-29).

Verses 43-54 identify the temple servants who returned. The temple servants were an order of Israelites who assisted the Levites. David was responsible for their creation (cf. 8:20). They are referred to as the Nethinim ("dedicated ones") in 7:24. The presence of several foreign names shows that this guild was primarily made up of foreigners. It is possible that they were descendants of the Gibeonites whom Joshua had enslaved (cf. Josh. 9:27). It is also possible that they were prisoners of war who were given to service of the temple. Numbers 31:25-47 describes this tradition. These Nethinim needed to faithfully worship Yahweh and follow the obligations of the Mosaic covenant, including circumcision. Ezekiel preached strongly against the use of "foreigners, uncircumcised in heart and uncircumcised in flesh" in the sanctuary (Ezek. 44:6-8). The temple servants were the lowest class of temple personnel.

Verses 55-58 identify the descendants of Solomon's servants who returned. They were likely foreigners who were enslaved by Solomon and appointed to serve in the temple. The total in verse 58 includes both the temple servants and the descendants of Solomon's servants, a fact which signifies the close relationship between these two groups.

The List of Those without Proof of Ancestry (2:59-63)

This section identifies those individuals who could not prove their ancestry. Evidently, the rest of the individuals named in this list could provide proof of their citizenship. This proof would likely have consisted of a genealogy tracing one's heritage to one of the sons of Israel. These genealogies were also used to exclude those with foreign blood. Although the individuals named here could not prove their ancestry, they were still allowed to return with the rest of the exiles. It is probable that they lost proof of their heritage during the chaos that surely existed during the Babylonian invasion and subsequent exile. They were probably given the same rights as circumcised foreigners. The phrase "who came up" in verse 59 is a repeat of the phrase used in 2:1, signifying that the cities mentioned here were located in the region of Babylonia where the exiles lived. The exact location of these cities is unknown.

Verses 61-63 reveal that even some priests were unable to prove their ancestry. These men were not allowed to serve as priests until the high priest could determine whether they were legitimate. He did this by using the Urim and Thummim. The exact nature of the Urim and Thummim is one of the great mysteries of the Old Testament. It has been suggested that they were two small objects which were used to signify the will of God, much like the casting of lots. Josephus contends that the answer was given by a miraculous shining of the jewels on the high priest's garments (*Antiquities of the Jews* 3.8.9). Evidently, at least one of these families, the sons of Hakkoz, had their claim upheld since Meremoth the son of Uriah is identified as a priest in Ezra 8:33 and as the grandson of Hakkoz in Nehemiah 3:4. The case of Barzillai was particularly difficult since he had taken the name of his wife, who was evidently not of a priestly family. This may have been done to become the family's heir. This would have entailed a renunciation of his priesthood since priests were forbidden from having an inheritance in the land (cf. Num. 18:20).

There was an inherent danger in unqualified priests performing the temple rituals as the story of Korah amply illustrates (Num. 16). Korah was to serve as an example of the sacredness of the priestly duties. Numbers 16:40 states that "no man who is not of the descendants of Aaron should come near to burn incense before the Lord, that he might not become like Korah and his company."

The governor mentioned in verse 63 is probably Sheshbazzar rather than a Persian official already in Jerusalem. It is quite doubtful that a Persian official would have been concerned about Jewish ceremonial religious practices. The governor restricted these priests from eating the "most holy things." The reference here is to the food that priests ate after performing their cultic services (cf. Lev. 2:3). The actions of the governor here support the view that this is Sheshbazzar rather than Zerubbabel. Since this is a cultic question, one would assume that Jeshua the high priest would have taken responsibility for the matter as opposed to Zerubbabel the governor.

The Sum Total of Returnees (2:64-67)

The total number of those who returned with Zerubbabel was 49,897 (Nehemiah records 49,942; cf. Neh. 7:66-67). This number does not correspond with the sum of the various groups mentioned in the chapter (i.e., 29,818). It is possible that women and children were not included in the initial numbers but were included in the final tally. However, this seems to be a very low number of women and children when compared to the number of men. Perhaps the difficulties of the journey and the uncertainty of what awaited them in Judah caused many women and children to remain in Babylon. It is also reasonable to assume that not all families are listed in the individual tabulations. A final possibility is scribal error, which is much more common in numerical lists.

Verse 65 informs us that many of the Jews had servants. The separation of these servants seems to suggest that they were regarded as property rather than as part of the congregation itself. It is highly probable that the vast majority of these servants were foreigners. The servants comprise about one-seventh of the total number of returnees. Obviously, the Jews had prospered in Babylon despite the rigors of the exile. The singers mentioned in verse 65 also speak to the prosperity of the remnant. They were not listed among the temple singers so this group was probably made up of paid entertainers. The prosperity alluded to here would not last long. Haggai, writing less than twenty years later, informs us that the remnant suffered a series of droughts because they did not have the proper attitude toward the rebuilding of the temple (Hag. 1:8-11). These droughts would have quickly consumed the wealth of the returned remnant.

The People Return to Their Cities (2:68-70)

The returnees contributed to the rebuilding of the temple by donating money to the effort. The remnant was probably inspired to take up this collection by the example of their forefathers at the building of the Tabernacle (Ex. 25:1-8). This collection added to the assistance provided by Cyrus and by the Jewish neighbors mentioned in 1:6. The "drachma" mentioned here is either the Persian daric or the Greek drachma. It is much more likely to be a reference to the Greek coin. The Greek drachma was far more common and was used throughout the Babylonian empire. It is doubtful that the Jews in Babylon would have had widespread access to Persian darics prior to the fall of Babylon. The "mina" is the Babylonian mina, a common silver coin. It was equal to 1/60 of a talent or 60 shekels. The phrase "according to their ability" in verse 69 is reminiscent of Paul's words in 2 Corinthians 8:3. In this passage Paul writes that the churches of Macedonia gave "according to their ability, and beyond their ability."

The remnant returns initially to Jerusalem and then many went to their ancestral properties. Once again, the text notes that the Jews were the rightful owners of the cities of Judah (cf. "their cities"). Those groups mentioned in verse 70 probably lived in the city of Jerusalem and the small towns near it while the rest of the remnant lived throughout Judah.

Study Questions
1. The priests were the descendants of whom?
2. What is the difference between a priest and a Levite?
3. What two guilds of Levites are identified in this list?
4. Who were the temple servants?
5. How many Jews returned with Zerubbabel?
6. What two types of coins are mentioned in verse 69?
7. Create your own list of those in your church who have proven faithful to the Lord.

Chapter 7
The Building of the Altar
Ezra 3:1-6

—⟨⟩—

Preview:

The first order of business for the returned remnant is the rebuilding of the altar. A rebuilt altar meant the restoration of the sacrificial system. And the sacrificial system was the avenue by which the returned remnant could receive the blessings of God.

As mentioned previously, there is a close connection between this chapter and the one preceding it. They are meant to be understood as a unit. The phrase "when . . . the sons of Israel were in the cities" in 3:1 alludes back to the final verse of chapter two which ended with "all Israel in their cities." The record of those who originally returned to the land in chapter two is not simply a list inserted into the text; it is an important part of the narrative.

While chapter two described the return of the Jews from exile, this chapter describes the nation's activities when they first enter the land. The first order of business for the returned remnant is the reestablishment of proper Yahweh-worship in the land. The foundational element in Yahweh-worship was the sacrificial system. The restored remnant naturally begins with the building of an altar. Without an altar it is impossible to offer sacrifices. This was also a way to thank the Lord for restoring them to the land. Abraham built an altar to the Lord immediately after entering the land for the first time (Gen. 12:7). Joshua likewise built an altar to the Lord after entering the land following the Exodus (Josh. 8:30-31). Here the restored remnant follows the example of their forefathers and immediately build an altar to the Lord upon entering the land.

The Nation Gathers in Jerusalem (3:1)

The activity of chapter two begins in the seventh month. This is the month Tishri (late September and early October) according to the Jewish calendar. The months of Nisan (late March and early April) and Tishri were the most important months in the Jewish year. The month of Nisan contained the Passover (Nisan 14), the Feast of Unleavened Bread (Nisan 15-21), and the Feast of Firstfruits (Nisan 16). The holy days in the month of Tishri included the Feast of Trumpets (Tishri 1), the Day of Atonement (Tishri 10), and the Feast of Booths, also named Tabernacles (Tishri 15-21). This fact helps us to narrow the time of year when the exiles returned to the land of Israel. One would assume that if the nation had been in the land during the month of Nisan then they would assuredly have celebrated the great holidays in that month, especially the Feast of Unleavened Bread, one of the three required holidays for all male Jews (along with the Passover and Feast of Booths; cf. Deut. 16:16). Hence the remnant had not yet returned by the month of Nisan.

It is likely that the returning exiles would have traveled during the spring, probably leaving Babylon early in the month of Iyyar (also called Ziv; late April and early May) and arriving in Jerusalem in the month of Tammuz (late June and early July). In this scenario, the nation would have avoided travel during the most difficult times of the year, that is, the cold winter, the early spring, which included the latter rains and the flood season, and the hot summer. The only major holiday from Nisan to Tishri is the Day of Pentecost, also called the Feast of Weeks, occurring fifty days after Passover on Sivan 7. Since all male Jews had to journey to Jerusalem for the Passover it can be assumed that the remnant had not yet returned to Israel by this date. It is likely that Passover occurred while the nation was traveling. So the first holidays that occurred after the nation entered the land are those in the seventh month, that is, Tishri. The year is probably 537 B.C., although a year before or after is entirely possible.

By the time of the seventh month the remnant had returned to their own cities (according to the scenario above they would have had two months to rebuild their homes and otherwise get settled in). The nation now returns to Jerusalem to offer thanks to their God by rebuilding the altar and celebrating the great feast days, including the Feast of Booths, the third of the required holidays for all male Jews. This would have been the first required holiday since their entrance into the land.

The Altar Rebuilt (3:2-3)

Jeshua and Zerubbabel work together to rebuild the altar. This is the only passage in the Bible where the name of Jeshua precedes Zerubbabel. This phenomenon is almost certainly because this section deals with the reinstitution of worship, the responsibility of the priests. There is no mention here of Sheshbazzar, a fact which suggests that he may have died. Jeshua and Zerubbabel receive help in the rebuilding project as the text notes the aid of both the priests and the laity. The term "brothers" utilized here should not be seen as identifying literal siblings. Rather, it is used in the sense of "peers," the priests being the peers of Jeshua and the laity being the peers of Zerubbabel.

From Jeremiah 41:5 it can be assumed that a sort of makeshift altar was erected in Jerusalem after the destruction of the temple in 586 B.C. This altar surely paled in comparison to the Solomonic altar. When Nebuchadnezzar destroyed Jerusalem in 586 B.C., the majority of the artisans and craftsmen of Judah were carried to Babylon in exile. As a result, the magnificent temple built by Solomon lay in ruins without the requisite personnel (and resources) needed to rebuild it. Without the temple as their centerpiece of worship, the Jews' cultic devotion gradually deteriorated. While it is almost certain that a temporary altar still existed in Jerusalem (cf. 4:2), it was probably not according to the regulations of the Mosaic Law. A new altar needed to be built.

This new altar was built on the foundation of the previous one, that of Solomon's temple. This fact again shows the continuity between the returned exiles and their forefathers. Williamson elaborates,

It has been repeatedly demonstrated by archeological discoveries that the veneration of sacred sites persisted long after their physical destruction. In the present instance, the exiles, to say nothing of the later community of the writer's own day, would have been most anxious to ensure that they centered their cult on the precise spot where God had revealed that 'the altar of burnt offering for Israel' should be situated (1 Chr. 22:1). The literary patterning of the one building on the other in the second half of this chapter undoubtedly arose out of such convictions about the importance of the physical continuity between the two.[1]

This physical continuity between the first temple and the second temple further reveals the covenantal continuity between the generation of the first temple and that of the second. In other words, this community felt that they were obligated to be obedient to the covenants given to their ancestors. The author reveals this theme by consistently referring to the writings of Moses throughout this passage (cf. 3:2, 4, 5).

The phrase "for they were terrified because of the peoples of the lands" is somewhat enigmatic. Perhaps in order to build the new altar the remnant was forced to destroy the previous one that had been utilized by those Jews and Samaritans who lived in Jerusalem during the exile. The destruction of their altar would surely have infuriated these groups. This may account for the rift between those who returned from Babylon and those who remained in the land (cf. 4:1-5). A more likely possibility, however, is that the phrase provides the reason why the remnant was so eager to reinstitute the sacrificial system, that is, because they were afraid of their enemies. They needed the help of their God. At this point, this is a healthy sort of fear. It is a fear that drives the one who is afraid to be obedient to the will of God regardless of the circumstances, trusting in the Lord for help and protection. Unfortunately, this fear of their enemies will continue to grow, eventually causing the remnant to stop the rebuilding project (cf. 4:4). After the completion of the altar the nation once again begins the ritual of offering morning and evening sacrifices, being sure to follow the ordinances contained in the Law of Moses. They also begin to celebrate the various holidays prescribed by the Lord.

The Nation Celebrates the Feast of Booths (3:4)

The first holiday mentioned is the Feast of Booths. There is no mention in the passage of the Day of Atonement, celebrated the week before the Feast of Booths. There is likewise no mention of the Day of Atonement in Nehemiah 8 where the nation is once again pictured as celebrating the

85

Feast of Booths. Surely the Day of Atonement would have been observed on both occasions. It is possible that there is no mention of the Day of Atonement in either instance because both passages are emphasizing the celebration of the remnant. The Day of Atonement was a solemn day and as such it does not fit with the flow of the narrative. Therefore, it is not mentioned in either chapter. It is also possible that the Day of Atonement was not observed because the Ark of the Covenant was no longer in existence. The Ark of the Covenant was a necessary part of the Day of Atonement ritual since the blood of the sacrificed goat needed to be sprinkled on the mercy seat of the Ark. Without the presence of the Ark of the Covenant in the temple, the Day of Atonement lost its significance.

The nation congregates in Jerusalem to celebrate the Feast of Booths. The Feast of Booths was one of the most significant days in the Jewish calendar. As mentioned previously, it was one of the three feasts during which every male Jew was required to be in Jerusalem (Deut. 16:16). It was celebrated from Tishri 15 to Tishri 21. During this week the Jews were required to live in booths (i.e., tents) set up around Jerusalem. This was done to commemorate the wilderness wanderings of the Exodus generation. The text states that the remnant offered the sacrifices according to the daily requirements. A special sacrifice was offered each of the seven days of this feast (see Numbers 29:12-38 for the details on what was to be offered on each day). The first day of the feast was to be a day of rest as well as the day after the feast ended.

The Reinstitution of the Sacrificial System (3:5-6)

These verses allude to the reinstitution of the other sacrifices and festivals. The festivals which had fixed dates included the new moon celebrations, the Passover, the Feast of Unleavened Bread, the Feast of Firstfruits, the Feast of Weeks (Pentecost), the Feast of Trumpets, the Day of Atonement, and the Feast of Booths (Tabernacles).

The offerings associated with these holidays, coupled with the "freewill offerings," provided a continual burnt offering to the Lord. The sheer number of the sacrifices kept the fires of the altar burning continuously. The "freewill offering" was a voluntary sacrifice that could be offered to the Lord whenever an individual felt led to do so. This was the only sacrifice that non-Israelites were allowed to offer to the Lord. The animals prescribed for this sacrifice included a male bull, a ram, and a he-goat. The poorest of the land were permitted to offer a turtledove or young pigeon without regard to sex. The freewill offering, with the exception of the skin, was entirely consumed upon the altar. It symbolized the complete surrender to God of an individual or congregation.

The reinstitution of the sacrificial system on the part of the returned remnant began on the Feast of Trumpets, the first day of the seventh month (Tishri 1). The section closes with the statement that the foundation of the temple had not yet been laid. This phrase introduces the next major section of the book, that is, the rebuilding of the temple. Even though the altar had been rebuilt and the sacrificial system had been reinstituted, the work was not yet complete. The Lord wanted the entire temple rebuilt (cf. Hag. 1).

Study Questions
1. Why was it important for the returned remnant to rebuild the altar?
2. What are the two most important months in the Jewish calendar? Why?
3. Which three holidays require the attendance of all male Jews in Jerusalem?
4. Why does the name Jeshua precede Zerubbabel in this passage?

5. Why was the remnant so eager to reinstitute the sacrificial system?
6. Why isn't the Day of Atonement mentioned in this passage?
7. Why did the Jews live in tents during the Feast of Booths?
8. What is a "freewill offering?"

Chapter 8
The Building of the Foundation
Ezra 3:7-13

—⊷⊶—

Preview:
The second order of business for the returned remnant is the building of the foundation of the temple. This was the first step in rebuilding the temple itself, the primary goal of the first half of the book of Ezra.

The Preparations for the Project (3:7)

The Jews prepare for the building of the temple's foundation by hiring masons and carpenters, two groups of artisans whose skills were essential to the project. The word "masons" refers specifically to stonecutters. These skilled laborers were hired with money, probably taken from the treasury referred to in 2:69. It can be assumed that these were foreigners since they had to be hired (cf. 1 Chr. 22:2).

Following the example of Solomon (cf. 2 Chr. 2:16), the remnant contracted the Phoenicians to bring timber from the region of Lebanon to the port city of Joppa. The Phoenicians were paid with food, drink, and oil just as they had been during the time of Solomon. In 2 Chronicles 2:10 the food given to the Phoenicians takes the form of wheat and barley while the drink consisted of wine. The oil was assuredly olive oil both in Solomon's day and in the present passage. The Phoenicians were in dire need of these dietary staples due to the lack of arable land in Lebanon. The land of Lebanon was not completely barren, however, as it was a perfect habitat for growing magnificent cedar trees. These cedar trees are legendary throughout the Old Testament. They are consistently used as the epitome of the world's strength, surpassed only by the Lord power (e.g. Psa. 29:5; Isa. 2:13; Amos 2:9; Zech. 11:2).

The Phoenicians are referred to by their principal cities Tyre and Sidon. Tyre is located on the shores of the Mediterranean Sea, about twenty miles south of Sidon and about seventy-five miles north of Joppa. It originally consisted of two parts, a rocky coast defense of great strength on the mainland, and a city on a small but well-protected island, about half a mile from the shore.[1] The two parts were eventually joined by a causeway constructed by the army of Alexander the Great while they were laying siege to the city in 332 B.C. Paul stayed in Tyre for a week near the end of his third missionary journey (Acts 21:3-4). Both Tyre and Sidon were included in the territory allotted to the tribe of Asher (Josh. 19:28-29). Several of the prophets announce the future destruction of Tyre and Sidon (e.g. Isa. 23; Ezek. 26; Joel 3:4-8; Amos 1:9-10; Zech. 9:1-4). Sidon is also situated on the shores of the Mediterranean Sea. Paul visited the city on his journey to Rome (Acts 27:3). The most noteworthy Phoenician in the Old Testament is Jezebel, the daughter of a Sidonian king (1 Kin. 16:31). King Ahab of the Northern Kingdom of Israel married Jezebel and introduced Baal worship into the land. He built a temple and altar to Baal in

Samaria (1 Kin. 16:32). He also built a shrine for Asherah, the consort of Baal (1 Kin. 16:33). The prophets Elijah and Elisha were called by God to speak against the worship of Baal in Israel.

The cedar logs purchased from the Phoenicians were taken by boat to the port city of Joppa. Joppa (Hebrew *yapo*; meaning "beauty") was located about thirty miles northwest of Jerusalem on the shores of the Mediterranean Sea. It was included in the territory allotted to the tribe of Dan (Josh. 19:46). Its harbor made it the port city for Jerusalem. Joppa is a popular city in the Scriptures. Here Solomon received the cedar logs for the temple in Jerusalem from Hiram (2 Chr. 2:16). Jonah boarded a boat sailing for Tarshish in Joppa (Jon. 1:3). And Peter raised Tabitha from the dead in the city, subsequently staying in the home of Simon the Tanner where he saw the vision of the great sheet (Acts 9:36-10:16).

Permission for the acquisition of cedar logs from the Phoenicians had been granted by King Cyrus himself. It is likely that Cyrus needed to approve this transaction because it involved multiple provinces in the Persian Empire. Fensham elaborates, "The author wants to point out that the delivery of cedar wood for the temple was approved by Cyrus. We must keep in mind that we have here a transaction between two different provinces in the Persian Empire, and permission for it had to be granted by the satrap of the Trans-Euphrates in the name of the King."[2]

The Overseers of the Project (3:8-9)

The remnant begins to rebuild the foundation of the temple in the second month of the second year following their return from Babylon. The second month in the Jewish calendar was the month Iyyar (late April and early May). The year is probably 536 B.C., nearly 70 years after the first exiles were taken to Babylon (605 B.C.). The second month was the perfect time of the year to start a building project.

It is the beginning of the dry season and the great holidays of Nisan have been completed. This was also the month in which Solomon began building the first temple (cf. 1 Kin. 6:1).

The leaders of the project are Zerubbabel and Jeshua. Although Sheshbazzar is not named here, he evidently had a hand in the project since he is credited with it in Ezra 5:16. As mentioned earlier, Sheshbazzar may have died by this time. Therefore, his part in the project may have involved the securing of the funds necessary to do the work (cf. 1:5-11). Since the project could not have been completed without the necessary financing, Sheshbazzar is given full credit in Ezra 5:16. However, in this passage we see that it is actually Zerubbabel and Jeshua who guide the project.

The priesthood assumes the role of overseeing the project. This is to make sure that the project was ritually correct. All Levites above the age of twenty were given administrative responsibility. Evidently, the age of twenty was now regarded as the age at which the Levites could take on responsibility (cf. 1 Chr. 23:24; 2 Chr. 31:17). Originally, the age had been set at twenty-five (cf. Num. 8:24; the age was set at thirty for those who carried the Tabernacle [cf. Num. 4:3, 23, 30]). Perhaps the minimum age was lowered because the total number of Levites kept declining. This would ensure that there were enough Levites to fulfill the temple duties. Take note that the text is once again careful to distinguish between the laity, the priests, and the Levites.

The Completion of the Project (3:10-11)

These verses describe the celebration of the people following the completion of the work. This celebration is led by the religious leaders, the priests and the Levites. The priests were clothed in their priestly attire and played trumpets. The Levites accompanied with cymbals. This celebration is reminiscent of those described in the book of Chronicles. Allen elaborates,

The description of the service is like accounts of temple worship in Chronicles. In both pieces of literature there is an imaginative reconstruction in terms of a later form of worship. From 2 Chronicles 5:12 and 7:6 we learn that the priestly trumpeters stood in front of the altar of burnt offering, opposite the Levitical singers, who faced the altar. The trumpeters sounded a signal, here presumably for the service to start, while the Levitical musicians evidently clashed their cymbals to announce the start of the hymn quoted in verse 11.[3]

This celebration was done according to the directions of King David, the one who had initiated music as an indispensable part of Jewish cultic worship. This celebration echoes that of 2 Chronicles 5:13 where the congregation is pictured singing "He indeed is good for His lovingkindness is everlasting" while accompanied by trumpets and cymbals. This refrain is used throughout the Psalter (cf. 100:5; 106:1; 107:1; 118:1; 136:1). The word translated "lovingkindness" is the Hebrew word *hesed*. This word is often used in reference to the covenants and can be translated "covenant love." Perhaps the best translation is "loyal lovingkindness," a phrase that vividly illustrates the Lord's commitment to His unconditional covenants.

The Twofold Response of the People (3:12-13)

Although the majority of the people viewed this day as a time of celebration, many in the audience viewed it as a time of mourning. The mourning was done by those who had seen the original temple before it had been destroyed by Nebuchadnezzar in 586 B.C. These men could see that this second temple would never compare to the glorious temple of Solomon. This scene is echoed in Haggai 2:3 where Haggai asks a series of questions, "Who is left among you who saw this temple in its former glory? And how do you see it now? Does it not seem to you like nothing in comparison?" This is also the reference of Zechariah's piercing question "For who has despised the day of small things?" (Zech. 4:10). The weeping of these old men is drowned out by the rejoicing of the youth. As a result, those who witnessed this event could not distinguish between the two. Once again, these verses (3:7-13) consistently allude to the actions of David and Solomon, either explicitly or implicitly, thereby showing continuity between this generation and their forefathers.

Study Questions
1. What two groups of workers do the Jews hire at the beginning of this passage? Why are they needed?
2. Where do the Jews get the timber needed for the building project?
3. What are the two principal cities of Phoenicia?
4. Who is a noteworthy Phoenician in the Old Testament?
5. What city served as a port for Jerusalem?
6. How old did the Levites have to be in order to have administrative responsibilities?
7. What Hebrew word is translated "lovingkindness?"
8. Why do some of the people mourn after the foundation of the temple is completed?

Chapter 9
The Response of the Enemies
Ezra 4:1-5

—∞∞—

Preview:
>   The successful projects of the returned remnant did not make everyone happy. This passage describes the response of the foreign inhabitants of the land, inhabitants who did not take kindly to losing their positions of influence in the province.

With the progress of the rebuilding project comes the antagonism of those who had previously controlled the land of Israel. This section builds on the previous chapter by detailing the response of the neighbors to the efforts of the Jews. One might anticipate that the foreigners of the land would be hostile to the growing Jewish influence in the province. By this time, they had lived in the province of Judah for decades, many perhaps being born in the land of Israel. Now, a group they currently regarded as "foreigners" was taking their land and influence away. Much like the modern-day Palestinians have resisted the actions of the United Nations in allowing the Jews to return to Israel, here the resident aliens resist the decision of the Persian king.

The Request of the Enemies (4:1-2)

Upon learning of the early success of the Jews in their rebuilding project the neighbors of the remnant approach the workers and ask if they can help in the effort. These neighbors of the Jews are identified as "enemies" with their very first appearance in the narrative. As a result, their subsequent request should be seen as a veiled attempt to hinder the work of the remnant rather than as a sincere request to join the project. The mention of the tribes of Judah and Benjamin in the first verse should be regarded as a case of synecdoche, the part being used for the whole (see the comments on Ezra 1:5).

The neighbors of the returned remnant had been brought to the land of Israel by Esarhaddon and other kings of Assyria. Originally, Sargon brought in the colonists from a number of Mesopotamian towns when the city of Samaria fell in 722 B.C. (cf. 2 Kin. 17:24). Additional colonists were later brought in during the reigns of Esarhaddon (680-669 B.C.) and Ashurbanipal (669–626 B.C.). The foreign policy of the Assyrians involved the exile of vanquished nations and the transplantation of foreigners into the conquered territories. This was done in hopes of preventing rebellions throughout their vast empire. The mixture of different cultures, languages, and religions made a unified rebellion nearly impossible. It must be remembered that at this time victorious nations did not have the resources to leave a standing army in each of the regions they conquered. As a result, they had to resort to other measures in an effort to control their subjects. Deportation served as the most severe of these techniques.

The foreign policy of the Assyrians, and subsequently the Babylonians, would eventually have a dramatic effect on the ethnic and religious population of the land of Israel. The foreigners transplanted to Israel intermarried with the Jews who had remained in the land. Although most of the Jews had been deported, and still more had journeyed to Egypt under Johanan, there was still a significant number of Jews who were left in the land. It has been estimated that the remnant of Jews who remained in Judah during the Babylonian exile numbered about twenty thousand souls.[1] This remnant managed to eke out a meager existence as farmers and herdsmen.

The offspring which resulted from the union of unfaithful Jews and heathen colonists became known as the Samaritans,[2] a mixed breed in both race and religion. The religion of the Samaritans was a syncretistic blend of the Hebrew form of Yahwehism instituted by Jeroboam and the pagan mysticism brought in by the colonists. This syncretistic form of worship was denounced by Ezra and Nehemiah with the result that the Samaritans were excluded from the worship activities performed in the temple. The Samaritans, led by Sanballat, erected a sanctuary on Mount Gerizim (near the ancient town of Shechem) in 409 B.C. following the expulsion of Manasseh from Jerusalem by Nehemiah. They also instituted their own priesthood (most of the Levites remained in Jerusalem) and regarded the Pentateuch alone as authoritative.[3] The rift between the Jews and the Samaritans continued throughout the intertestamental period. During the time of Christ, the Jews and Samaritans had little social and commercial contact (cf. John 4:4-9).

Those who had been transplanted to Israel by the kings of Assyria quickly began to worship Yahweh, the God of the land in which they now lived (2 Kin. 17:25-28). Jeremiah 41:5 confirms the claim of the foreigners that they had continued sacrificing to the Lord even after the fall of Jerusalem in 586 B.C. However, the worship of the Lord on the part of these foreigners was not according to the Mosaic Law as the text notes that they continued to serve their own gods (2 Kin. 17:29). Since the priest who had been chosen to teach the original foreigners the religious practices of Yahweh-worship had previously been taken into exile (2 Kin. 17:27), it can be assumed that he was a priest of the syncretistic worship of the Northern Kingdom as opposed to that of Jerusalem. This worship involved the worship of Yahweh but accommodated the inclusion of other cultic practices (such as the erection of golden calves). Consequently, even the worship of Yahweh that had originally been taught to the ancestors of this current generation of foreigners had been tainted. It was further polluted by the fact that they continued to serve other gods in addition to Yahweh. True worship of Yahweh demanded allegiance to Him alone (Ex. 20:3). This current generation of foreigners does not truly seek the God of Israel as they claim in verse two.

The Reply of the Remnant (4:3)

Since the worship of the foreigners was not genuine, the remnant did not allow them to help in the project. The remnant, led by Zerubbabel and Jeshua, quickly reject the request of the foreigners. There is a bit of diplomacy, however, in their rejection as they appeal to the original decree of Cyrus which only granted the right of rebuilding the temple to those who returned from exile. Williamson elaborates,

> The reason they gave was, strictly speaking, quite correct: it was they, and they alone, whom Cyrus had authorized to build the temple; cf. 1:2-4. The self-confessed foreign origin of those asking to help was sufficient, on political grounds, to bar them from participation. As the form of Tattenai's subsequent inquiry shows, they might have jeopardized the whole undertaking if they had not kept to the letter of the authorization granted them. This was why they insisted, somewhat misleadingly, that their work was

a direct and uninterrupted continuation of what had been started in Sheshbazzar's time; cf. 5:16.[4]

The Result of the Rejection (4:4-5)
The rejection of the foreigners on the part of the remnant served to inspire them to try to stop the project. Their initial actions were threefold. First, they discouraged the remnant. This technique would have consisted of the mocking, heckling, and otherwise taunting of the workers. This was also the first method employed in future years by Sanballat and Tobiah when they were trying to discourage the rebuilding efforts of Nehemiah's men (Neh. 4:1-3). Second, they frightened the remnant. This approach would have involved threats to the remnant, perhaps endangering their lives. There was little the Jews could do to protect themselves. The supply lines from Tyre and Sidon were long and unguarded. The small remnant was surrounded on all sides by their enemies. They were completely vulnerable. This method was likewise used by Sanballat and Tobiah in Nehemiah's day (Neh. 4:7-11). Third, the foreigners hired counselors to frustrate the men of Israel. The exact nature of this course of action is unknown. It is probable that the "counselors" are in fact Persian officials. The resultant meaning would thus indicate that the foreigners bribed the Persian authorities to frustrate the rebuilding project. Bribery was a frequent practice in ancient times among the Persians (Josephus, *Antiquities* 11.2.1).

The subversive tactics of the foreigners persisted until the reign of the Persian King Darius. This king is to be identified as Darius I Hystaspes (522-486 B.C.). Therefore, the opposition continued throughout the rest of the reign of Cyrus (until 530 B.C.), and during the entire reigns of Cambyses (530-522 B.C.) and Pseudo-Smerdis (522 B.C.). As verse 24 notes, the plan of the enemies was a rousing success. The remnant eventually stopped working on the temple, a condition that would continue for sixteen years.

Study Questions
1. Why do the enemies of the Jews offer to help rebuild the temple?
2. In what year did the city of Samaria fall to the Assyrians?
3. Why did the Assyrians exile the peoples they conquered?
4. Who were the Samaritans?
5. Did the foreigners truly worship Yahweh?
6. Why does the remnant reject the request of the foreigners?
7. What is the response of the foreigners to this rejection?

Chapter 10
Further Attempts to Stop the Project
Ezra 4:6-24

—∞∞—

Preview:
Get out your Persian history books; you're going to need them for this section! These verses describe the efforts of the enemies to thwart the work of the Jews from the time of Darius until Ezra's day. The problem is, Ezra simply changes time periods by referring to different kings. Without knowledge of these kings and the dates of their reigns, this becomes one of the most confusing chapters in the Bible.

This section is a parenthesis in the flow of the narrative. Ezra, in an attempt to illustrate some of the measures used by the enemies of the Jews, interjects into the story three events that occur more than fifty years after the events of 4:1-5. These events evidently reminded him of the lengths to which the opposition was willing to go in their repeated efforts to stop the Jews from achieving success.

The Attempt in the Days of Xerxes (4:6)

The Persian King Ahasuerus identified here is better known by his Greek name Xerxes. Ahasuerus was his Hebrew name, a translation of the Persian name Khshayarsha. Xerxes reigned over the Persian Empire from 486 to 465 B.C. Esther married Xerxes and became the queen of Persia after he deposed Vashti, also known as Amestris. During his reign the enemies of the Jews wrote a letter to the king containing accusations against the Jews who lived in Judah and Jerusalem. The accusations contained in this letter were probably the same ones mentioned in 4:13-16. Evidently, nothing happened as a result of this attempt.

The First Attempt in the Days of Artaxerxes (4:7)

Artaxerxes, whose name means "having a kingdom of justice," was the third son of Xerxes and Amestris. He reigned over the Persian Empire from 464-424 B.C. Ezra led a return to Israel during his reign and Nehemiah served as his cupbearer. During his reign the enemies of the Jews again tried writing a letter to the Persian king in an attempt to stop the Jews from rebuilding their city. The identities of Bishlam, Mithredath, and Tabeel are otherwise unknown. The term "colleagues" (Aramaic *Kenat*) used here occurs eight times in the next 48 verses. It refers to the various associates of the referent, likely including secretaries, lawyers, minor officials (cf. 5:6), and military personnel used as bodyguards. No details are supplied about the contents of this letter. Perhaps it was similar or even identical to the one described in 4:11-16. Again, it seems as if nothing happened as a result of this attempt.

Parenthesis: The Use of Aramaic in Ezra

Ezra 4:8-6:18 is written in Aramaic. So too is 7:12-26. Aramaic is a northwest Semitic dialect. It became the lingua franca of the Ancient Near East due to the abundance of Aramaean merchants in the region. The Jews who settled at Elephantine in Upper Egypt spoke and wrote in Aramaic. Christ Himself spoke Galilean Aramaic. Daniel 2:4-7:28 is the only other section of the Old Testament written in Aramaic.

There is an obvious reason for most of the Aramaic in Ezra. It is mainly comprised of copies of official correspondence, for which Aramaic was the customary language. 52 of the 67 verses fall into this category. The other 15 verses serve as connecting passages. There are two main views as to the reason for this occurrence. First, the Aramaic material may be extracted from an Aramaic history of the period. In this case, the entire section would have been copied from a single source document. Second, since the original readers of Ezra obviously knew Aramaic, the author simply keeps the connecting passages in Aramaic to avoid transitioning from one language to another. Either view is equally plausible.

The Second Attempt in the Days of Artaxerxes (4:8-23)

At some point subsequent to the writing of the letter mentioned in 4:7, Rehum writes a second letter to King Artaxerxes on behalf of the enemies of the Jews. The exact date of this letter cannot be ascertained, though it must have been written between 458 (the date of Ezra's return to Jerusalem referred to in verse 12) and 444 B.C. (the date of Nehemiah's return to Jerusalem and subsequent rebuilding of the walls of the city). One would assume that Ezra would have wanted to begin work on the walls of the city immediately upon his return so a date closer to 458 is to be preferred. Although other names are given, Rehum should be viewed as the primary author. Shimshai served as his amanuensis.

Rehum is identified as a "commander." The exact nature of this position is unknown. He may have been a satrap. However, if he was a satrap then the absence of this common title is striking. It is more likely that he was a high official in the province, perhaps directly under the satrap.

The names listed in verse nine are supplied to lend weight to Rehum's assertions and to give the impression of unity on the part of the inhabitants of the land in their opposition to the Jews. The "judges" were probably royal judges concerned with matters of state. The "lesser governors" were likely governors of the smaller cities within the province. Erech is a region of Mesopotamia. Susa was the capital of Elam before becoming the winter capital of the Persian Empire (see comment on Esther 1:2).

The Osnappar referred to in verse ten is Ashurbanipal, king of the Assyrian Empire from 669-626 B.C. His father was Esarhaddon, the Assyrian king referred to in 4:2. Around 645 B.C., Ashurbanipal invaded the territory that included Erech and Susa, evidently exiling some of the inhabitants to the region of Samaria (cf. 4:9). The "River" is to be identified as the Euphrates River. The entire phrase "beyond the River" refers to the Persian province named Trans-Euphrates.[1] This province stretched from the Euphrates River to the border of Egypt, thereby encompassing the whole of Syria and Palestine.

The actual letter written by Rehum is supplied in verses 11-16. The phrase "the Jews who came up from you" in verse twelve is a reference to the return of Ezra and his party in 458 B.C. This collection of exiles was the second known group to return to the land of Israel from Babylon. Note also the use of the term "Jews." This term became the common name of the people of Israel after their exiles throughout Assyria and Babylon (cf. Neh. 1:2; Esth. 2:5; Dan. 3:8). It is the shortened form of the phrase "one from Judah." The reference to walls and foundations in this verse shows the initial attempt on the part of the Jews to rebuild the walls of the city. This project would eventually be successfully completed by Nehemiah. Note that the enemies refer to the city of Jerusalem as "rebellious" and "evil." They will later defend this description (4:15). The letter to Artaxerxes by Rehum contained two accusations against the Jews. The initial accusation is revealed in verse thirteen. Rehum informs Artaxerxes that the Jews will stop paying tribute if the walls are successfully rebuilt. This would have resulted in the king's honor being tarnished (4:14). Taxation was an important part of the Persian Empire (see comment on 2:1-4). The taxes are identified as "tribute, custom, or toll." The exact nature of each of these three taxes is unknown.

Verse sixteen reveals another accusation. Rehum warns Artaxerxes that he will lose the entire province of Trans-Euphrates if the walls of Jerusalem are successfully rebuilt. This assertion is based on Jerusalem's long history of rebelling against foreign nations (cf. 4:15, 19). The Southern Kingdom of Judah had rebelled against the Assyrians in the days of Hezekiah (2 Kin. 18:7). They rebelled against the Babylonian King Nebuchadnezzar in the days of Jehoiakim (597 B.C.; 2 Kin. 24:1). And finally, they again rebelled against Nebuchadnezzar in the days of Zedekiah (588 B.C.; 2 Kin. 24:20).

Artaxerxes' reply is given in verses 17-22. Artaxerxes addresses his reply to Rehum, Shimshai, and the rest of their colleagues. Artaxerxes begins his letter by informing Rehum that the letter sent by him was "translated and read" to the king. Evidently, Artaxerxes did not understand Aramaic and needed to have the letter interpreted.

Artaxerxes next details the steps he took upon hearing the interpretation of the letter. To his credit, Artaxerxes carefully researched the claims of Rehum (4:19-20). After a thorough search of the Assyrian and Babylonian annals, the king discovered that Jerusalem did indeed have a long history of rebelling against their Suzerains. He also discovered that some of Jerusalem's kings had been quite powerful. This seems to be a reference to David and Solomon (and perhaps even to Uzziah and Hezekiah). If Jerusalem had been that powerful in the past, it could certainly rise to prominence again in the future, thereby posing a threat to the Persian Empire and Artaxerxes himself. As a result, the king issues a decree calling for the Jews to halt their rebuilding efforts.

The wording of the decree, however, supplies the king with an out. He writes, "until a decree is issued by me." King Artaxerxes wisely leaves the door open for a change of mind since the decrees of the Persians could not be repealed once they became official (cf. Esth. 1:19; 8:8; Dan. 6:8). In fact, the decree contained in 4:17-22 represented a sort of change of his earlier decree giving Ezra virtually unlimited freedom to do as he wished (cf. 7:21). Artaxerxes would subsequently change his mind one last time, allowing Nehemiah to return in 444 B.C. to complete the walls of Jerusalem.

The leaders of the opposition, no doubt thrilled at the king's reply, hurry to stop the rebuilding efforts of the Jews. The text notes that this was done "by force of arms." Perhaps the Jews would not stop the work until forced to do so by armed soldiers.

The Project is Halted (4:24)

The narrative now picks up where verse five left off. The repetition of the phrase "the reign of Darius King of Persia" unites this verse with verse five. The plan of the enemies was a rousing success. This verse supplies two pieces of information which were lacking in verse five: First, the fact that the remnant stopped working on the temple (536 B.C.); And second, the fact that this condition continued until the second year of the reign of Darius (520 B.C.), a total of sixteen years.

Study Questions

1. What is the Greek name of Ahasuerus?
2. Who is Shimshai?
3. Who is Osnappar?
4. What is the name of the river alluded to in 4:10?
5. The letter of Rehum is written in what language?
6. What two adjectives are used by the enemies of the Jews in reference to the city of Jerusalem?
7. What are the two accusations made against the Jews by Rehum in his letter?
8. What is the reply of Artaxerxes to the letter of Rehum?

Chapter 11
The Project is Restarted
Ezra 5:1-5

Preview:
Throughout the Old Testament, whenever the people of the Lord proved unfaithful, the Lord raised up prophets to show them the error of their ways. Such is the case in this passage. This time, the prophets Haggai and Zechariah are used by the Lord to motivate His people to restart the work on the temple.

The Ministry of Haggai and Zechariah (5:1-2)

The time frame for these verses is supplied in 4:24. It is now the second year of the reign of Darius I (520 B.C.). The Lord who had "stirred up" the spirit of Cyrus (1:1) and the spirit of those who originally returned to the land (1:5) now speaks to the remnant through His prophets. Both Haggai and Zechariah claim that their words came directly from the Lord (cf. Hag. 1:1; Zech. 1:1).

The name Haggai means "festival" and the name Zechariah means "Yahweh remembers." Zechariah was the son of Berechiah and the grandson of Iddo. Since Ezra identifies him simply as the son of Iddo it is possible that his father Berechiah had already died. As a result, Ezra would be indicating that Zechariah succeeded Iddo in the priesthood. It seems more probable, however, that Zechariah is mentioned as the son of Iddo not to identify his parentage but to identify him as a member of the priestly family of which Iddo was the head (cf. Neh. 12:16). This would account for the absence of a reference to Haggai's father in this passage. Iddo is identified in Nehemiah 12:4 as one of the priests that returned from exile with Zerubbabel. Both prophets supply a considerable amount of information about the rebuilding project in their prophetic books.

Haggai sharply criticizes the remnant for living in "paneled" houses while the temple was still in ruins (Hag. 1:4). The Jews had not simply stopped work to put up their own homes. The use of this word implies that improvements had been made to their dwellings. He further reveals that the remnant was engaged in extensive agricultural endeavors and economic pursuits (Hag. 1:6). Each of these demonstrates the skewed priorities of the remnant. Essentially, the message of the prophet is to give God's interests the priority over their own interests. Even the great leaders of the remnant were not above blame. Haggai specifically addresses his message to Zerubbabel and Jeshua (Hag. 1:1). The prophets Haggai and Zechariah support the Jews in their rebuilding efforts for almost five years until the temple is finally completed.

The Response of Tattenai (5:3)

Immediately upon hearing the news that the Jews have resumed work on the temple, the governor of the province of Trans-Euphrates approaches the remnant and questions them regarding the project. His chief concern was assuredly whether or not these actions involved subversion. The Persian Empire had been teeming with revolts since the death of Cyrus and especially since Darius took the throne. These revolts were common in ancient times. There was always a period of uncertainty whenever a change in the monarchy occurred. Vassal nations frequently used this opportunity to rebel against their Suzerain.

The name of the governor is Tattenai. His name may be a shortened form of the Babylonian name *Nabu-tattanu-uşur*, meaning "Nabu protects him you gave."[1] There is extra-biblical evidence of his existence. A Babylonian record dated 502 B.C. speaks of a Tattenai governor of Ebernari. Ebernari was another name for the province of Trans-Euphrates. Tattenai appears to have been accountable to a still higher official named Ushtani who was responsible for the combined satrapy of Babylon and Ebernari.[2] Shethar-bozenai was likely the governor's assistant.

It was the provincial governor's duty to question the activity of the Jews. His responsibilities included the protection of the Persian king. From his point of view, it was entirely possible that the Jews were rebuilding portions of their city as part of a subversive plot to rebel against the Persians. As detailed in the previous section, the Jews had a history of rebelling against their Suzerains. While Tattenai himself should not be regarded as an enemy of the Jews, he was likely informed of their efforts by those who were.

Another reason for Tattenai's concern may have been the Jewish expectations of their coming Messiah. This Messiah was to rescue His people from bondage and build an empire from which He would rule the earth (e.g. Isa. 9:6-7; 11:1-16; Jer. 23:5-6; Dan. 2:44; 7:13-14; Mic. 5:2-4). In recent years predictions concerning the coming King were becoming more and more common. With each of these predictions the expectations of the Jews were heightened. This expectation was surely known to the Persians. And the Persians were well aware of the accuracy of the Jewish prophecies (cf. Isa. 45:1).

Zechariah himself fuels the speculation concerning the coming Messiah with his prophecies concerning the "Branch." According to Zechariah, this "Branch" will "build the temple of the Lord" and then "rule on His throne" (Zech. 6:12-13). Jeremiah adds that the coming "Branch" will "reign as king" (Jer. 23:5). Naturally, these prophecies would not have pleased the Persian king currently ruling over Israel, especially since both prophets currently ministering in Judah single out Zerubbabel as being specially chosen by God (cf. Hag. 2:23; Zech. 4:6-9).

For these reasons, then, the provincial governor demands the credentials of the remnant. He wants to know by what authority they are rebuilding the temple. Although the text does not inform us of the fact here in verse four, the governor also asks for the names of the leaders so that he can report them to the king (cf. 5:10).

The Resolve of the Jews (5:4-5)

Evidently the Jews could not produce the credentials necessary to prove their right to rebuild the temple. The returning exiles must have had some original documents when they first returned to the land, possibly including a copy of the decree of Cyrus. It can be assumed that they would have needed to show these documents to the officials in Trans-Euphrates upon arriving in the province. Apparently, these credentials had been lost. Perhaps they had been destroyed by the enemies of the Jews. Whatever the reason, the remnant could not prove their right to rebuild the temple. The governor needed to investigate their claim. The text notes that the remnant continues the building project while awaiting the reply of the king.

The phrase the "eye of their God" was upon them is worthy of note. The Lord who had "stirred up" the spirit of Cyrus (1:1) and the spirit of those who had originally returned (1:5) and had spoken to the remnant through His prophets (5:1) was continuing to watch over and direct His people. Psalm 33:18 says "Behold, the eye of the Lord is on those who fear Him, on those who hope for His lovingkindness." The Hebrew word *hesed* ("lovingkindness") often refers to the Lord's commitment to His covenantal promises (cf. Deut. 7:9, 12; 1 Kin. 8:23; 2 Chr. 6:14; Neh. 1:5; 9:32; Ps. 25:10; 89:28; Isa. 54:10; Dan. 9:4). The remnant is trusting in the Lord's lovingkindness (the Lord has promised to rebuild the temple; cf. 1:2), therefore the "eye of their God" is upon them.[3]

Study Questions
1. What date is the second year of Darius I?
2. What is the meaning of the name Haggai?
3. What is the meaning of the name Zechariah?
4. Who is Tattenai?
5. Give two reasons for the concern of Tattenai.
6. Do you believe the "eye of your God" is upon you? Why or why not?

Chapter 12
The Letter of Tattenai
Ezra 5:6-17

Preview:

Tattenai, the Persian official introduced in the previous passage, wrote a letter to King Darius investigating the claims of the Jews. Pay special attention to the actions of both Tattenai and Darius in this book. Although both are foreigners, they prove faithful to their God-given responsibilities.

Since the Jews could not prove their right to rebuild the temple Tattenai takes pen in hand to write to the king requesting him to research the official records. Ezra provides the reader with a copy of the letter sent by Tattenai to King Darius of Assyria. Although the exact date of this letter is not mentioned, various passages help us to narrow down the possibilities. It could not have been written prior to Elul 24 (September 21), 520 B.C., the day on which the Jews resumed the building of the temple after Haggai delivered his scathing rebuke of the remnant for stopping the project (cf. Hag. 1:15). It must have been written prior to Adar 3 (February 19), 515 B.C., the day on which the temple was completed (cf. 6:15). Taking into account the length of time needed for the letter to reach the Persian king, for him to research its claims, for his response to reach Tattenai, and for the Jews to complete the temple, the letter could not reasonably have been written after 517 B.C. Therefore, any date between September 21, 520 B.C. and the end of 517 B.C. is possible with a date near the end of 520 B.C. the most preferable.

The Actions of Tattenai (5:6-10)

Tattenai begins the letter by announcing that he had discovered that the Jews were rebuilding the temple of the "great" (Aramaic *rab*) God. Since this reference is made by an unbeliever, it seems best to translate this word as "chief" or "head." This rendering would see the word as a title rather than as an attribute. Tattenai notes that this temple was being built with considerable strength and with great care. Special emphasis is given to the size of the boulders being used; obviously, the larger the stones the greater their strength. The phrase "huge stones" literally means "rolling stones" and indicates boulders too large to move by any other means. The mention of timber reveals that this temple was being built following the same techniques employed by Solomon. In fact, Ezra 6:4 prescribes the same ratio of stone to timber (three to one) as that utilized by Solomon (1 Kin. 6:36). This technique of laying timber between layers of stone or brick was common in the Ancient Near East and was probably used as a means of strengthening buildings against earthquakes.[1] The overall quality of the building likely added to Tattenai's concern that this project could be part of a subversive plot against the king.

Tattenai is careful to record his own actions in questioning the remnant concerning the legal means by which they had undertaken this project. He further adds that he questioned the remnant concerning the identities of the leaders. The names ascertained by Tattenai are not supplied in the letter. This is a glaring omission since the text notes that Tattenai requested the names so that he might relay them to the king (5:10). While it is possible that Ezra intentionally deleted the names, it seems more likely that Tattenai was withholding the names until he heard from the king concerning the validity of the claims. One would expect that Zerubbabel and Jeshua were at the top of the list.

The Answer of the Jews (5:11-16)

Tattenai next informs the king of the remnant's response. The Jews once again identify their God as "God of heaven" (see note on 1:2). The Jews refer back to the previous temple built by the "great king" Solomon. It was this temple which Cyrus' decree had allowed to be rebuilt (cf. 5:13). In fact, the temple was to be rebuilt "in its place" (5:15), that is, in the very spot that it had originally stood.

The response of the Jews demonstrates that they are well aware of the reason for their exile. They fully acknowledge that their ancestors had provoked the Lord to wrath by worshipping other gods (cf. Ezek. 23; Hos. 2:1-13). As a result the Lord punished their disobedience by scattering them among the nations (cf. Lev. 26:33; Deut. 28:64) and allowing their temple to be destroyed (cf. 2 Chr. 7:20-22). Although Nebuchadnezzar was the human agent who systematically deported the Jews to Babylon (605, 597, 586 B.C.) and destroyed Solomon's temple (586 B.C.), the Jews realize that it was really God who allowed it to happen ("He [God] gave them into the hand of Nebuchadnezzar").

The Lord still granted favor to His chosen people, however, as He "stirred up the spirit" of Cyrus (1:1) to issue a decree allowing the Jews to return to their land and rebuild their temple (1:2-4). The Jews also noted the fact that Cyrus returned the articles of the temple which had been taken by Nebuchadnezzar, further proof that he had authorized the rebuilding project. Cyrus is identified in verse thirteen as the "king of Babylon." Although unusual, this title for Cyrus is not without precedent. In fact, Cyrus refers to himself as the king of Babylon in the Cyrus Cylinder.[2] The title is used here to contrast with and denote his power over "Nebuchadnezzar king of Babylon" (5:12).

The reference to Cyrus here also serves a literary purpose. Allen explains, "The report of the history of the temple project serves for the reader as a flashback to the narrative of the Cyrus-backed mission in chapter 1. We are reminded that the present rebuilding is the long-awaited fulfillment of that mission. Chapter 6 will bring its own reminder of the first chapter, but even now the narrator draws an arc of literary coherence, spanning the lapse of a score of years."[3]

Sheshbazzar is given credit in verse sixteen for laying the foundation of the temple. As mentioned earlier, Sheshbazzar's part in the project may have involved the securing of the funds necessary to do the work (cf. 1:5-11). Since the project could not have been started without the necessary financing Sheshbazzar is given full credit in this letter. However, from other passages we see that it is actually Zerubbabel and Jeshua who are primarily responsible for the success of the project (cf. 3:8-11). It is also possible that Sheshbazzar is identified because he would have been the individual named in the Persian records.

The Request of Tattenai (5:17)

The letter closes with a request that the claims of the Jews be verified. Tattenai expects that the matter will be resolved with a search of the king's records in Babylon (cf. 5:17). Time will show that the supporting documents will actually be found at a remote fortress in Media called Ecbatana (6:2). The final line of the letter is a request for the king's instructions concerning the entire matter. Tattenai wanted to know if the claims of the Jews were accurate and if so, whether or not Darius wanted to allow the project to continue. Note the difference between this letter by Tattenai and the letter penned by Rehum in 4:11-16. Rehum's letter was obviously biased and full of false accusations while Tattenai's letter fairly and accurately described the events as they occurred.

Study Questions
1. What is the meaning of the Aramaic word *rab*?
2. What is the ratio of stone to timber used by both Solomon and the restored remnant?
3. Why was this ratio used?
4. Why did the Lord send the Jews into exile?
5. Why is Cyrus called the "king of Babylon?"
6. What are your impressions of Tattenai?

Chapter 13
The Actions of Darius
Ezra 6:1-12

———∞∞∞———

Preview:

In the first chapter, the decree of Cyrus was instrumental in allowing the Jews to return to the land of Israel. Here, the decree of Darius is going to be instrumental in allowing the Jews to finish their temple.

The Discovery of the Decree of Cyrus (6:1-5)

Having received the letter of Tattenai, King Darius issued a decree calling for a search of the official Persian records to verify the claims of the Jews. The search began in the city of Babylon. Evidently, Darius assumed that since the returned remnant had originated in Babylon, then that was where the decree must have been made. Darius was no doubt aware that Cyrus had stayed in Babylon for a period of time following his conquest of the city. However, a record of the decree was not found in Babylon.

As it turns out, a scroll containing the original decree of Cyrus was found at the fortress of Ecbatana, the summer capital of the Persian kings during the reign of Cyrus. Xenophon informs us that Cyrus lived in Babylon during the winter, in Susa during the spring, and in Ecbatana during the summer (*Cyropaedia* 8.6.22). Ecbatana (modern Hamadan) was located in the province of Media and was the capital of the Medes until they fell under the control of Cyrus. Cyrus had stayed in Ecbatana in the summer of his first year as king of Babylon, the same year he originally made the decree allowing the Jews to return to Jerusalem and rebuild their temple.

The decree of this passage is similar to that of the first chapter; however, there are some notable differences. These differences do not necessarily mean that there were two different decrees.[1] However, they probably do indicate two different sources. The edict of 1:2-4 was probably a portion of the decree that heralds would have proclaimed in each city as they journeyed throughout the empire. This would have been a shortened form of the official decree suitable for posting. The decree of 6:3-5 was likely taken from the official records of the Persian king. The official records would have contained the full text of the original decree, thus detailing all of the particulars. Obviously, this document would have been much longer than the one quoted in 1:2-4. Only those portions that deal with the specifics of the temple are copied by Ezra. For example, there would have been no need to repeat the portions dealing with Cyrus' decree allowing the Jews to return to Jerusalem since they are already there.

The decree of this passage provides a few additional details concerning the actual building of the temple. First, the decree provides the exact dimensions of the temple, 60 cubits high and 60 cubits wide. A cubit is about eighteen inches in length. These dimensions called for the rebuilt temple to be twice as high and three times as wide as Solomon's temple (cf. 1 Kin. 6:2). Perhaps Cyrus wanted the glory of this temple to surpass that of Solomon's. Evidently, the Jews did not take advantage of this opportunity (cf. 3:12-13; Hag. 2:3). Second, the decree authorizes the use of "huge stones." The sight of these stones likely concerned Tattenai when he first inspected the building project since he specifically mentioned the "huge stones" being used in the construction (5:8). Third, the decree allows for the expenses incurred in the construction to be taken from the royal treasury. The offer to cover the expenses of this project fits well with what is known of Cyrus' policies regarding foreign religions. Fourth, the decree called for the return of the gold and silver temple utensils that had been taken by King Nebuchadnezzar. While the fulfillment of this portion of the decree was recorded in 1:7-11, it was not recorded in the decree itself (1:2-4).

The Instructions to Tattenai (6:6-7)

Having found the original decree of Cyrus, Darius now relays his instructions to Tattenai (cf. 5:17). The original decree of Cyrus is allowed to stand. Darius instructs Tattenai and his colleagues to refrain from interfering with the remnant's rebuilding project, in essence allowing the Jews to continue working on the temple, the "house of God." Once again, the text is careful to note that the temple is to be built "on its site" (cf. 5:15), an obvious reference to the site of the original temple built by Solomon. Tattenai is identified as the "governor" of the province of Trans-Euphrates while Zerubbabel is identified as the "governor" of the Jews. Darius apparently views Zerubbabel as subordinate to Tattenai.

The Decree of Darius (6:8-12)

Darius also offers a decree of his own. It is at once obvious that Darius has the help of a Jewish religious authority as he writes his decree. Darius' decree calls for five things. First, Darius orders the funds for the temple to be drawn from the royal treasury and paid to the Jews. The treasury alluded to here was that of the province of Trans-Euphrates. This treasury was probably located in Babylon. Second, Darius provides for the sacrificial system of the Jews to be restored. Bulls, rams, and lambs were the most valuable and important sacrifices in the cultic worship of the Jews. The decree also provides for a supply of wheat, salt, wine, and anointing oil. Third, Darius instructs the remnant to pray for him and his family. Once again, this is in keeping with Persian policy. The Cyrus Cylinder records a similar decree by Cyrus, "May all the gods whom I have placed within their sanctuaries address a daily prayer in my favor before Bel and Nabu, that my days may be long." According to Herodotus, it was customary among the Persians to utter a prayer for the king whenever a sacrifice was offered (*Histories* 1.132).

Fourth, Darius reveals the punishment that is to be given to anyone who violates his decree. This punishment takes the form of poetic justice. If anyone harms the house of God, then his own house will be destroyed. The lawbreaker would also receive retribution. The form of this retribution is debated. The Aramaic literally reads "and lifted up he shall be smitten upon it." This phrase could be a reference to flogging (e.g. NEB).[2] Taken this way, the punishment would involve tying the criminal to a beam and beating him. This beating would not necessarily result in the loss of the criminal's life. The phrase could also refer to impalement (e.g. NASB, NKJV, NIV, NRSV). In other words, the offender was to be impaled on a timber from his own house. Obviously, this judgment would take the life of the lawbreaker. The second option is much more likely, especially in light of the ultimate destruction of the offender's house. It was to be made into a refuse heap (lit. "dunghill"). If the guilty party was still alive at this point, one would expect him to attempt to rebuild his house. Fifth, Darius calls on the Lord to invoke divine judgment on all who attempt to destroy the rebuilt temple. This invocation is in the style of an ancient Near Eastern curse formula. Fensham elaborates,

> The curse formula was used throughout ancient Near Eastern history to protect what was regarded as precious, e.g., the sarcophagus of a king. It was also used to protect a treaty. The overturning of a king meant the overturning of his throne, as we know from the curse formula. In the Bagistan Inscription Darius invoked the hostility of Ahuramazda [his favorite god] against anyone who would destroy the inscription.[3]

Study Questions

1. Where was the scroll containing the decree of Cyrus found?
2. What additional details concerning the actual building of the temple are supplied in this passage?
3. List the five things called for in the decree of Darius.
4. What was to happen to those who disobeyed the decree of Darius?
5. Do you believe that Darius will be in heaven? Why or why not?

Chapter 14
The Completion of the Temple
Ezra 6:13-22

‒‒‒‒‒∞∞∞‒‒‒‒‒

Preview:
The moment has finally arrived. Thanks to the efforts of Cyrus, Sheshbazzar, Zerubbabel, Jeshua, Haggai, Zechariah, Tattenai, and Darius, the temple is finally finished. It is indeed a time to celebrate the *hesed* of the Lord.

The Impact of the Decree of Darius (6:13-15)

Immediately upon receiving the instructions of Darius, Tattenai rushes to make sure the wishes of the king are carried out. It is worthy of note that the same Aramaic expression, translated "with all diligence," is used to describe the building efforts of the remnant (5:8; translated "with great care"), the urgency of the king's decree (6:12), and the actions of Tattenai and his colleagues in carrying out that decree (6:13).

The leaders of the Jews were successful in their efforts largely due to the efforts of Haggai and Zechariah. These prophets revealed the "command of the God of Israel." The Lord's will was accomplished through the use of the Persian kings Cyrus, Darius, and Artaxerxes. Although Artaxerxes has not yet played a role in the rebuilding efforts, he will issue a decree allowing Nehemiah to return to the city of Jerusalem and rebuild its walls (cf. Neh. 2:3-8).

The temple was completed on Adar 3 (February 19), 515 B.C., four and a half years after the remnant restarted the project and twenty-one years after they had laid the foundation. The temple was rebuilt seventy years after it had been destroyed (i.e., 586 B.C.). Solomon's temple stood for almost 400 years. This temple will stand for almost 600 years (until Titus destroys it in A.D. 70).

The Impact of the Temple on Israel

At this point, the importance of the temple must be discussed. The Jews were quite unique in the Ancient Near East because they were monotheistic. All of the nations surrounding Judah were polytheistic. The Jews worshipped a single God, namely Yahweh, and believed that He was intimately involved in their daily personal and national existence. They viewed their successes and failures, both personally and nationally, as a direct consequence of their faithfulness or disobedience to their God. As a result, the place where they worshipped Yahweh, the temple, became the most significant symbol of the restored community.

Along with its importance as a religious institution, the temple played an important role in the political, economic, and social spheres of Jewish culture. Blenkinsopp asserts that "the decisive political event in the establishment of a viable Jewish community in the homeland was the rebuilding of the temple and organization of its cult."[1] The cost of maintaining the temple was obtained by means of the tithes of the people as well as an annual levy of one third of a shekel (Neh. 10:32). The sacrificial system itself took a considerable toll of livestock, grain, and other commodities, including wood.[2] This system would soon become an overwhelming burden for the population, with the result that many either stopped offering sacrifices or offered sacrifices of low quality (cf. Neh. 13:10-11; Mal. 1:8, 13; 3:8-10). The social rifts present in the Jewish community were exacerbated with the rebuilding of the temple. Those who controlled the temple in Jerusalem exercised political control over the entire Trans-Euphrates region. The successful rebuilding of the walls of the city would serve to further intensify the rift between the Jewish community and the foreigners, including Samaritans, living in the region.

Not only did the presence of the temple cause a rift between the Jews and Samaritans, it caused a rift within Judah itself. The temple system, and consequently the cultic worship performed there, became the means by which to obtain social and economic status within the Jewish community at large. Blenkinsopp explains,

> Comparison with other "temple communities" throughout the empire, especially in Mesopotamia and Asia Minor, suggests that they [Jewish temple community] thereby constituted themselves as a distinct entity within which participation in, and of course active support of, the cult were closely linked with social and economic status within the province. Effective control of the "redemptive media," in effect the sacrificial system, translated into social control, including the ability to dictate terms for qualification as members of this entity. It is this situation more than anything else which created the conditions for the emergence of sectarianism in the Second Temple period.[3]

As Blenkinsopp mentions, the temple system was the single most important cause for the emergence of sectarianism in Judaism. The most notable sects that emerge by the time of the New Testament are the Pharisees, Sadducees, and Scribes.

The Dedication of the Temple (6:16-18)
The Jews celebrate the completion of the temple by having a ceremony of "dedication." The Aramaic word used here is *hanukah*. This word will eventually lend its name to an annual festival commemorating the re-consecration of the temple after its defamation at the hands of Antiochus Epiphanes (Chislev 25, 167 B.C.). The celebration was held "with joy," a theme repeated at the end of these verses when the remnant celebrates the Feast of Unleavened Bread "with joy, for the Lord had caused them to rejoice" (6:22).

As part of the celebration, the Jews offer 100 bulls, 200 rams, 400 lambs, and 12 male goats. This was certainly a significant sacrifice for the impoverished remnant; however, it pales in comparison to the 22,000 oxen and 120,000 sheep offered in dedication to Solomon's temple (1 Kin. 8:63). Note the offering of twelve male goats as a sin offering for "all Israel." Leviticus 4:22-24 prescribes the offering of a male goat as a sin offering. Each tribe of Israel was represented in this offering. There are no so-called "lost" tribes. Although the majority of the remnant was comprised of men of Judah, Benjamin, and Levi, there assuredly were members of every tribe present in the restored community. Notice also that the text identifies the remnant as the "sons of Israel" as opposed to "Jews" (6:16, 21).

The sons of Israel are once again divided into three categories; the priests, the Levites, and the laity (cf. 1:5; 2:70; 3:8). The text also again notes that the restored remnant was careful to follow the instructions of Moses. The "book of Moses" gave specific instructions concerning the various duties of the priests and Levites (cf. Ex. 29; Lev. 8; Num. 18). David was responsible for instituting the "divisions" and "orders" (cf. 1 Chr. 23-24).

The Celebration of Passover (6:19-22)

It is at this point that the language of the narrative reverts back to Hebrew. The Passover was the first Jewish feast day to be celebrated in the completed temple, occurring five weeks after the dedication of the temple. Passover was celebrated on Nisan 14, the "fourteenth of the first month." Each household sacrificed a one-year-old unblemished lamb at twilight on this special day (Ex. 12:6). The lamb is then eaten with unleavened bread and bitter herbs (Num. 9:11). The Passover holiday commemorated the Lord's redemption of the nation of Israel from bondage in Egypt.

The identification of "all those who had separated them-selves from the impurity of the nations of the land" is prob-lematic. It is possible to see these as proselytes (gentile converts) who had returned to the land of Israel from Babylon with the Jews. It is also possible that these were Jews who had remained in the land throughout the exile but had now separated themselves from the foreign peoples. The first option seems best in light of the strong terminology used in 4:1-3 of the neighboring community.

The Feast of Unleavened Bread began on the day following Passover and lasted seven days (Lev. 23:6-8). During this week, the Jews were forbidden from eating leav-ened bread (Deut. 16:3). The first and seventh days were to be days of rest (Ex. 12:16). This festival commemorated the hasty departure of the Jews from Egypt.

The identification of Darius as the "king of Assyria" is noteworthy. The Persian kings have now been identified as the "king of Persia" (1:1, 2, 8; 3:7; 4:3, 5, 7, 24; 6:14), the "king of Babylon" (5:13), and the "king of Assyria" (6:22). The title is probably used here to denote the reversal of the foreign policy of the Assyrians. The Persian kings, having conquered the Assyrians and Babylonians, are now in a position to right the wrongs committed by those kings.

These verses are the climax of the first half of the book. The nation is now resettled in the land and proper worship of Yahweh has been restored. The hero of the story is God. The narrative of the first half of the book begins when the Lord "stirred up the spirit" of the Persian king (1:1) to allow the Jews to return to the land of Israel and ends when the Lord "turned the heart" of the Persian king (6:22) to encourage the Jews to finish the temple.

Study Questions
1. On what day is the temple completed?
2. How many years were the Jews without their temple?
3. Why was the temple so important to the Jews?
4. How many animals are sacrificed as part of the celebration?
5. Who was responsible for instituting the "divisions" and "orders?"
6. Which holiday is celebrated by the nation in this passage?
7. What does this holiday commemorate?
8. What were the Jews forbidden to eat during the Feast of Unleavened Bread?

Chapter 15
The Introduction of Ezra the Scribe
Ezra 7:1-10

―――ᴄᴔᴔᴑ―――

Preview:

The second half of the book begins with an introduction of the main character in the rest of the narrative, Ezra the priest and scribe. This amazing man "set his heart to study the law of the Lord, and to practice it, and to teach His statutes and ordinances in Israel" (7:10). As a result, God gave him a significant ministry.

Ezra's Genealogy (7:1-5)

The phrase "now after these things" introduces a significant shift in the narrative, effectively separating the events of chapters 7-10 from those of 1-6. The events of these chapters take place during the reign of Artaxerxes, almost 58 years after the events of chapter six. In the meantime, the events of the book of Esther took place in Susa. It is unknown how many, if any, returns took place in these intervening years.

The name Artaxerxes means "having a kingdom of justice." The Artaxerxes referred to here should be identified with the first king of that name, Artaxerxes I. Artaxerxes I was the third son of Xerxes and Amestris and reigned from 464-424 B.C. Nehemiah was his cupbearer. An alternative view is that this Artaxerxes should be identified as Artaxerxes II. Artaxerxes II reigned from 404-359 B.C. This view is based on Ezra 10:6, which reports that Ezra went to the chamber of Jehohanan the son of Eliashib. Johanan is identified as the grandson of Eliashib in Nehemiah 12:22. Since Eliashib was the high priest during the time of Nehemiah, his grandson must have lived much later. Although this view is popular in modern research, it rests on shaky ground. Fensham explains,

> First, no proof whatsoever exists that the Johanan mentioned in Ezra 10:6 is the same person as the grandson of Eliashib. Indeed, Eliashib could have had more than one son, and one of them could have been called Johanan, for this was a fairly common name in the fifth century. Second, this hypothesis is built on the assumption that the mentioning of Nehemiah in the Ezra memoir and the reference to Ezra in the Nehemiah memoir must be regarded as later insertions when the Chronicler became confused about the chronological sequence of the two men. Such a mistake so close to the history it describes is extremely unlikely.[1]

This scene introduces us to the main character of the second half of the book, that is, Ezra the priest and scribe. The name Ezra means "help" and may be a shortened form of the name Azariah, meaning "the Lord has helped." The text supplies an extensive genealogy for Ezra, thus revealing the considerable importance of this man. The first ancestor named is Seraiah, who witnessed the fall of Jerusalem (2 Kin. 25:18). Despite the length of Ezra's genealogy, it fails to reveal the line from Seraiah to Ezra, perhaps consisting of four or five individuals. It is possible but highly unlikely that Ezra is of the line of Jehozadak and Jeshua. Jehozadak, the son of Seraiah, was carried to Babylon by Nebuchadnezzar. Jeshua returned with Zerubbabel and served as the high priest for the original returnees. If Ezra was of the line of Seraiah-Jehozadak-Jeshua, then his failure to mention these names is shocking. It is also possible that Ezra was the actual son of a different Seraiah, which may account for the omission of names between the two Seraiahs. There is another noticeable gap in the genealogy. There are six names omitted between Azariah and Meraioth (cf. 1 Chr. 6:3-15). The omission of names in biblical genealogies is common. The phrase "son of" can simply mean "descendant of."

Since the line is traced to Aaron the chief priest, the primary reason for the genealogy seems to be to identify Ezra as a priest, thereby giving him the authority to institute various reforms. Several noteworthy names occur in the list. Aaron of course was the first High Priest and principal aide to his brother Moses. Eleazar assisted at the commissioning of Joshua (Num. 27:18-23). Phinehas is famous as the priest who speared both the Israelite and the Moabite woman he was having sex with in Numbers 25. It is also probable that he penned the final verses of the book of Joshua (24:29-33).

Ezra's Return to Jerusalem (7:6-9)

Ezra journeyed from Babylon to Jerusalem in the seventh year of King Artaxerxes (458 B.C.). The phrase "went up" is a traditional idiom used to describe a journey to Jerusalem. The idiom is a reference to the fact that Jerusalem sits at the top of a mountain (e.g. 2 Chr. 36:23; Ezra 1:3; Isa. 2:3). Ezra is identified as a "scribe." This term indicates that he was skilled in the interpretation of the law. Ezra's role as a scribe would certainly have added to his abilities as a priest. Throughout the rest of the narrative, the scribe's reforms should be seen as rooted in a thorough examination of the Scriptures. The use of the word "scribe" here might also have a double meaning. Fensham explains,

> In the first place it refers to a Persian office. Ezra was appointed by Artaxerxes for the specific task of acting as secretary in Judah on behalf of the religious institutions. He was also a priest, however, who had made a special study of the law of Moses, the legal parts of the Pentateuch. He was thus able to interpret the law for the Jewish community. Some scholars hold that Ezra as a scribe and learned man in the law was the compiler and final editor of the law. But there is in Ezra and Nehemiah nothing to prove this surmise. It is much better, and true to these books, to accept that Ezra must be regarded as the founder of Jewish exegesis on the method of the *midrash halakha*. He was thus an interpreter par excellence.[2]

Prior to the second temple period, scribes usually served as little more than secretaries, writing down the king's decrees and keeping a record of the events that occurred during each reign (cf. 2 Kin. 22:10; 1 Chr. 24:6; see also Ezra 4:8). Their access to the monarch also meant that they often served as the king's confidants, messengers, treasurers, or even military commanders (cf. 2 Kin. 18:17-19:7; 25:19; 2 Chr. 24:11; 26:11). Beginning with Ezra, the position of scribe takes on far more importance. Scribes were now primarily students of the Law who were responsible for copying, writing, and teaching. By the time of the New Testament, scribes wielded significant power throughout Israel.

The primary duties of a scribe were threefold. First, they served as the copyists of the law. This duty also involved the interpretation of the law. When the law did not speak to a specific case then the scribes created precedent. As a result, they in effect became legislators creating new law. Second, they served as the teachers of the law. It was their duty to make sure that every Israelite was acquainted with the rules and regulations of the law. Third, they served in a judicial capacity, passing sentence in the court of justice. Their knowledge of and skill in interpreting the law made them ideal candidates for the position of judge. Scribes were routinely found among the ranks of the Sanhedrin.

Ezra is further identified as "skilled in the law of Moses," a phrase which denotes his wisdom and efficiency in the use of the biblical text. Note that the text ascribes the Law to Moses in 7:6, a verse that serves to argue against the claims of many modern critical scholars who hold to the documentary hypothesis (i.e., JEDP theory). This verse also argues for the authority of the Scriptures, claiming that they were given by the Lord God of Israel, a strong assertion of divine inspiration. The stipulations of the law were not the figment of a man's imagination; they were the very commands of God Himself.

In a classic example of foreshadowing, the text informs the reader that the king granted Ezra everything he requested. The fact that Ezra requested something of the king is never supplied in the narrative. It can be assumed that he requested the items granted to him in Artaxerxes' letter (7:12-26). The phrase "the hand of the Lord" (or God) is used extensively throughout chapters seven and eight (7:6, 9, 28; 8:18, 22, 31).

The trip from Babylon to Jerusalem took four months and covered roughly 900 miles. A direct trip from Babylon to Jerusalem would have covered around 500 miles but this route was strenuously avoided because of the Arabian Desert. Ezra's group would have followed the Euphrates River north, then journeyed west across the plains to Damascus, seat of the satrapal government, and finally south through Samaria to Jerusalem. This trip was quite dangerous, especially in light of a recent rebellion that had broken out in Egypt. The company left Babylon in Nisan (late March, early April) of 458 B.C. They planned to leave on the first day of the month, however, the need to recruit Levites delayed their start until the twelfth day (cf. 8:31), just two days before Passover. The repeated reference to the seventh year of King Artaxerxes in verses seven and eight serves to show that Ezra arrived in Jerusalem in the same year that he left Babylon. The group arrives on the first day of Ab (late August, early September) in 458 B.C. Ezra did not journey back to Jerusalem alone. Verse eight lists several groups that accompanied him. The details of this company are supplied in chapter eight.

Ezra's Ministry (7:10)

This is one of the most amazing verses in the entire Bible. The conjunctive "for" connects this verse to the preceding phrase "the good hand of his God was upon him." In other words, the reason the good hand of God was upon Ezra was because of the things described in this verse. As a result, this verse can be perceived as detailing a four-step formula for gaining the favor of the Lord. First, Ezra "set his heart." The scribe determined within his heart that he would faithfully and resolutely commit himself to the habits detailed in the rest of the verse. Second, Ezra studied the law of the Lord. The scribe devoted his life to the reading and analysis of God's Word. Third, Ezra practiced the law of the Lord. The scribe's examination of the scriptures was not simply a growth of knowledge. He applied that knowledge to his life. Fourth, Ezra taught the law throughout Israel. The scribe did not keep the things he learned to himself. He taught them to others. Kidner comments on this verse,

> He [Ezra] is a model reformer in that what he taught he had first lived, and what he lived he had first made sure of in the Scriptures. With study,

conduct and teaching put deliberately in this right order, each of these was able to function properly at its best: study was saved from unreality, conduct from uncertainty, and teaching from insincerity and shallowness.[3]

Study Questions

1. Which Artaxerxes is referred to in the first verse of chapter seven? When did he reign?
2. What does the name Ezra mean?
3. The line of Ezra is traced to what significant ancestor?
4. What is Phinehas famous for?
5. In what year did Ezra journey from Babylon to Jerusalem?
6. What were the primary duties of a scribe?
7. What is the four-step formula for gaining the favor of the Lord as described in 7:10?
8. Are you currently following this formula in your own life?

Chapter 16
Ezra's Commission from Artaxerxes
Ezra 7:11-28

Preview:

The benefactor of Ezra is the Persian King Artaxerxes. This is the same individual who will allow Nehemiah to return to Jerusalem and rebuild the walls of the city. As you think through the book of Ezra, be sure to note the impact of the Persian kings in the history of the Jews.

The Introduction to the Letter (7:11)

This verse should be regarded as an introduction to the king's letter. As noted earlier, Ezra made a request of King Artaxerxes. In response to Ezra's request, the king issued a decree granting Ezra everything that he requested (cf. 7:6). A copy of that decree is supplied by Ezra. Ezra is again identified as a priest and scribe. The text also once again emphasizes the fact that Ezra was a specialist in the laws and statutes given by Yahweh to the children of Israel.

The King's Permission (7:12-14)

The letter of Artaxerxes (12-26) is provided in Aramaic, the language of official correspondence in the Persian Empire. The decree gives Ezra, and whoever among the Israelites who wishes to join him, the opportunity to journey to Jerusalem. The decree also entrusts Ezra with the responsibility to enforce the law of Yahweh.

The letter begins with a typical salutation. The author of the letter, Artaxerxes, is identified first. Artaxerxes is referred to as the "king of kings," a popular designation in the Persian courts designed to describe the Persian king's sovereign rule over the entire earth. The recipient of the letter, Ezra, is identified next. Ezra is referred to as a priest and a scribe, evidently his official titles. The term translated "perfect peace" is a common Persian greeting.

The first item of business addressed in the letter is the permission of the king allowing the Israelites to return to Jerusalem. This return was not forced, only those who were "willing to go" had permission to return. This decree allowed all Jews to return to Jerusalem. While there were no doubt many Jewish colonies throughout the empire (e.g., Elephantine, Susa), the major concentration of Jews was in the region of Babylon. As is his custom, Ezra again separates the laity from the clergy (cf. 1:5; 3:2, 8).

Ezra is described as having been sent by "the king and his seven counselors." Evidently, when Ezra initially made his request, the king sought the advice of his supreme council. It was customary in the Ancient Near East for rulers to have a group of royal advisors. The Persian king's council was made up of seven princes (cf. Esth. 1:14). These seven princes were the only people permitted to enter the king's presence uninvited and unannounced (Herodotus, *Histories*

3.84). These men would occupy a counseling role similar to that of our president's cabinet members. The king's advisors were men who "understood the times" (Esth. 1:13). They were knowledgeable of the affairs of the empire and how the king's decisions would affect the people.

The King's Provision (7:15-20)

The second item of business addressed in the letter is the provision of the king for the temple of Yahweh, the God of Israel. The king offers silver and gold to Ezra dedicated to the purchase of animals and other offerings. He also allows the people to make freewill donations to the collection. These offerings were to be presented at the temple in Jerusalem. Any excess money was to be used at the discretion of Ezra, probably earmarked for the daily service of the temple. The king's accurate knowledge of the sacrifices acceptable to Yahweh almost assuredly originated with Ezra himself. In fact, as a scribe with some connections with the king, Ezra was likely involved in the actual writing of this letter.

The vessels referred to in verse nineteen are probably gifts from the king to the temple of God. It is doubtful, though possible, that they are original Solomonic temple utensils which had been overlooked when the temple vessels were returned by Cyrus. The section ends with the stipulation that Ezra had a right to draw on the royal treasury if anything else was required.

The King's Orders for the Treasurers (7:21-24)

The third item of business addressed in the letter is a decree given specifically to the king's treasurers. The treasurers of Trans-Euphrates are instructed to provide Ezra with whatever he requests. Ezra's rights of requisition were considerable but not unlimited, the king having provided a ceiling on each item. A hundred talents are almost four tons.

A hundred kors are about 650 bushels. A hundred baths are 607 gallons.

Verse twenty-three betrays the reason why Artaxerxes is so willing to aid Ezra; "lest there be wrath against the kingdom of the king and his sons" by the God of heaven. This is the negative of the same order given by Darius in 6:10. This verse reveals once again the religious policy of the Achaemenids based on the teachings of Zoroaster. The Persian kings did whatever possible to get the gods of the nations they controlled on their side (see comment on 1:2-4). This religious conviction might also have been influenced by the political state of the empire. Margalith explains,

In 460 B.C. the confederation of Greek cities under Athenian leadership known as the Attic-Delic League sent a fleet of 200 war galleys against Persia in the Cyriot seas. This fleet sailed to Egypt, gained a great victory over the Persian army there and captured Memphis in the autumn of 459. This placed the coast of Palestine and Phoenicia into Greek hands as the only possible route from Ionia to Egypt.

It was in 458, immediately after the fall of Memphis to the Greeks, that Ezra the Judean courtier was sent to Judea "to enquire concerning Judah and Jerusalem" (7, 14) and to reorganize and strengthen this traditional enemy of the Philistines. From the point of view of the Persian king a strong pro-Persian Judea was a major threat to the Greek coastal life-line, and as long as the Greeks dominated the coast and Egypt he supported a strong Judean province headed by a Judean-Persian official and peopled by a pro-Persian population, most of whose families were hostages in Babylon and Persia.[1]

Verse 24 reveals that the temple employees were exempt from paying tribute to the Persian king. The exemption granted to the Jewish religious personnel by the Persian king was certainly not an isolated case (Herodotus, *Histories* 3.91). Kidner elaborates,

> The inhabitants of the Greek island of Delos, when they fled at the approach of the Persian fleet in about 490 BC, were given an assurance of Darius's veneration for so sacred a spot, the birthplace of Apollo and Artemis; and the Persian general Datis made lavish offerings there. More significantly, the same King Darius I made specific mention of a long-standing royal policy in these matters in the course of a rebuke to one of his officials in Asia Minor. The official, Gadatas, had failed to exempt certain cult-servants, the "gardeners of Apollo," from paying tribute.[2]

The King's Orders for Ezra (7:25-26)

The fourth and final item of business addressed in the letter is a decree given specifically to Ezra. The phrase "wisdom of your God" is a reference to the Torah. This phrase reveals that the Torah is more than just a record of laws; it is revelatory instruction that comes directly from Yahweh. Ezra was officially responsible to teach the nation the commandments of God.

Ezra is instructed to appoint "magistrates and judges" throughout the province of Trans-Euphrates. It is possible that these terms are two names for the same position. However, it is just as likely that the terms are a reference to the two kinds of tribunals which existed in the Persian Empire. The Persians had a social tribunal which was responsible for routine matters of law and a royal tribunal which heard matters of state. It is likely that these terms are used here to designate religious judges as opposed to civil judges. Civil judges would have already been in existence. These religious judges were responsible for making sure that the laws and commands of Yahweh were adhered to. They were also responsible for teaching those laws to the people.

The authority granted to Ezra in these verses essentially makes him a sort of religious governor in the province. The phrase "all the people who are in the province" is a specific reference to the Jews who live in the province of Trans-Euphrates as opposed to a general designation including people from other nations. In other words, the king is not forcing everyone in the province to live according to Jewish religious law. He is, on the other hand, forcing the Jews to live according to the laws of their God. Ackroyd is among those who believe that the text does refer to the entire province, envisioning "a situation in which the whole province becomes one community, all obedient to the law."[3]

The letter concludes by granting Ezra (and his appointed judges) the authority to execute judgment on all Jews who refuse to obey the commandments of God and the "law of the king." This latter phrase is probably a reference to the specific decree of 7:12-26 as opposed to a general reference to the laws of the Persians. Ezra and his judges are given permission to punish lawbreakers in four ways. First, they can confiscate the offender's possessions. Second, the judges are able to imprison wrongdoers. Third, they can banish the evildoers from the province. Fourth, the judges can execute those who refuse to follow the law.

The Thanksgiving of Ezra (7:27-28)

These verses contain the words of Ezra and mark the first time the scribe speaks in the narrative. Note the use of the first person. While the use of the first person is common in Hebrew prophetic literature (cf. Jeremiah, Ezekiel, Habakkuk), it is quite peculiar in Old Testament historical narrative (Nehemiah is the only historical book written primarily in the first person).

Ezra, like Nehemiah, is quick to credit the Lord for the success he encounters. He realizes that the king granted his request because the Lord moved his heart. Ezra also realizes that the Lord strengthened him because the "hand of the Lord" was upon him (cf. 7:6, 9). This tribute takes the form of a doxology (declarative praise) similar to those found elsewhere throughout the Scriptures (cf. 1 Sam. 25:39; 2 Chr. 2:12; Ps. 144:1; Dan. 3:28; 2 Cor. 1:3; Eph. 1:3; 1 Pet. 1:3).

The text notes that the Lord moved the king's heart to "adorn" the temple in Jerusalem. The word translated "adorn" (Hebrew *pa'ar*) is the same word used by Isaiah to refer to the eschatological work of the Lord to "glorify" (Isa. 60:7) or "beautify" (Isa. 60:13) His sanctuary. It is possible that Ezra deliberately uses this word in reference to the temple to signify an initial fulfillment of Isaiah's prophecy. Note that in each passage the subject of the verb is the Lord.

Ezra further thanks the Lord for his "lovingkindness" to him personally in the midst of the Persian courts. The word translated "lovingkindness" is the Hebrew word *hesed*. Here it may simply mean "benevolence" or "goodwill." However, the word often carries the inherent meaning of "loyal lovingkindness" in the Old Testament, especially when applied to the Lord keeping His covenant (cf. Neh. 1:5; 9:32; Dan. 9:4). This may be a further indication of the fact that Ezra believes that his return is a partial fulfillment of the promises of the Lord to regather His people (Mic. 2:12; Zeph. 3:20; Zech. 10:10). The final fulfillment of these promises awaits the institution of the Millennial Kingdom following the Second Coming of the Messiah.

Ezra closes the section by revealing that he gathered some of the leading men of Israel to return with him to Jerusalem. Here we have an unfortunate chapter break. This final phrase is probably better seen as introducing chapter eight rather than closing chapter seven.

Study Questions
1. Why do you think Ezra consistently separates the laity from the clergy?
2. Why does Artaxerxes help Ezra?
3. Do you think you will see Artaxerxes in heaven? Why or why not?
4. In what four ways can Ezra punish lawbreakers?
5. How has the Lord shown *hesed* to you?

Chapter 17
Ezra's Journey to Jerusalem
Ezra 8:1-36

—∞∞∞—

Preview:

Ezra, having gained the permission of King Artaxerxes, now embarks on his trip to the holy city of Jerusalem. The trip will take four months, an abnormally long time. The main reason is because the wagons were loaded down with 30 tons of gold and silver provided by those who remained in Babylon, including the king himself.

The Roster of Returnees (8:1-14)

As mentioned previously, the end of 7:28 should begin chapter eight. In the second half of 7:28 Ezra mentioned that he gathered some of the leading men of Israel to journey to Jerusalem with him. These verses provide a roster of those families. The text indicates that the returnees departed from the city of Babylon.

Almost all of the Jews who returned were direct relatives of those who had returned almost eighty years earlier under the leadership of Sheshbazzar (cf. 2:3-15). The one exception is the family of Joab. This fact reveals the difficult nature of keeping families intact during the exile. Perhaps these Jews were among those who remained behind while supporting their relatives who returned with Sheshbazzar (cf. 1:4, 6).

The list begins with two priests. This is the reverse of the list in chapter two where the priests were listed after the laity. Another notable difference is that the priests of this chapter follow the Aaronite lineage while those of chapter two follow the Zadokite lineage. Phinehas was the son of Aaron's third son Eleazar while Ithamar was Aaron's fourth son (cf. Ex. 6:23-25). Also mentioned is a descendant of David, Hattush. Hattush is the grandson of Shecaniah and great-great-grandson of Zerubbabel (cf. 1 Chr. 3:17-22). This genealogy provides further proof for the early date of Ezra's ministry. A time gap of eighty years between four generations is natural. The text fails to supply the number of men who accompanied these individuals.

The Search for Levites (8:15-20)

Ezra assembled the company on the banks of the river that ran to Ahava. The exact location of this waterway is unknown. It was assuredly an irrigation canal, one of many that ran from the Euphrates to the Tigris, which flowed at a slighter lower elevation. These canals were often named after their destination. The party stays at this location for three days. It was evidently a good time to take stock and make sure that everything needed for the journey was at hand.

While they are encamped, Ezra realizes that there are no Levites in the assembly (for a description of the Levites, see the comment on 2:40-42). Sheshbazzar likewise had difficulty in finding Levites willing to return to Jerusalem (cf. 2:40-

42). Perhaps the tedious life of temple ritual was not particularly appealing. Ezra immediately takes steps to rectify this situation. After briefing them on their mission, Ezra sends a delegation of the leading men and two "teachers" to Casiphia to talk to Iddo, himself one of the elders of the Jews. The word translated "teachers" is better translated "diplomats" in light of the nature of their role in this situation. They were men renowned for their ability to persuade. The number and type of emissaries reveals the difficult nature of their task, which is trying to convince those who perform the service of the temple to return to their duties. The exact location of Casiphia is unknown. It was likely a district of Babylon. Evidently, there was a Jewish temple located there and Iddo served as its chief priest ("leading man"). It is unlikely that Iddo was an official ("leading man") over an entire district of Babylon. Fortunately, Iddo is able to provide the company with a small number of Levites. Sherebiah is singled out as a "man of insight," perhaps a reference to his abilities in the Law of Moses. Iddo is also able to supply a large group of temple servants (for a description of the temple servants, see the comment on 2:43-54). Ezra again attributes his success to the "good hand" of God (cf. 7:9). The text once again points out the role of King David in organizing the priestly families (3:10; cf. 1 Chr. 24:7). The number of those who returned with Ezra was about 1700 men plus women and children, perhaps a total of close to 5000 individuals.

The Spiritual Preparation (8:21-23)

Prior to leaving their encampment, Ezra calls on the assembly to fast. The motivation for the fast was to seek the Lord's protection for the journey. Ezra evidently realized that the trip to Jerusalem would be quite hazardous. Fasting commonly accompanies a time of great anxiety. Fasting, in a sense, is often involuntary. In other words, quite often individuals are too worried or anxious to eat food. Their stomachs are uneasy, resulting in a loss of appetite. David fasts while pleading for the life of his child (2 Sam. 12:16). The inhabitants of Nineveh fast upon hearing news of the imminent judgment announced by the Lord (Jon. 3:5). Nehemiah fasts upon hearing the bad news concerning the state of the city of Jerusalem (Neh. 1:4). And finally, King Darius fasts while Daniel is in the lion's den (Dan. 6:18). As an interesting side note, Ezra 8:21 was the text of John Robinson's last sermon at Leiden before the Pilgrims sailed for the New World in 1620.[1] The fasting of the assembly was accompanied by prayer (cf. 2 Chr. 20:3-12).

Ezra refuses to ask the king for an armed escort to protect the pilgrims on their dangerous journey. In those days the roads were teeming with gangs of bandits. Ezra's reason for not making a request is admirable. He refused to request a military escort because he had told the Persian king about the power of His God. Surely Ezra could not ask for the king's help when he had already told him that he was following the Lord's will. If it really was the Lord's will, then He would protect His people. This refusal to request an armed escort on the part of Ezra reveals his incredible faith, especially in light of the considerable amount of gold and silver they were carrying (cf. 7:15-16). Many scholars who hold to the unity of the books of Ezra and Nehemiah attempt to use these verses to show that Nehemiah was inferior to Ezra. Fensham explains,

> Some scholars want to see in these verses an apologetic tendency against Nehemiah, because he traveled with a military escort (Neh. 2:9). It is then regarded as a subtle hint of the superiority of Ezra over Nehemiah. But we can explain this difference of approach as follows. Ezra the priest went to Jerusalem on a religious mission. In such a case a military escort would have seemed strange, because the religious group would then have shown no faith

in their God. Nehemiah went as a political official, a governor, to Jerusalem. In such a case, the king would protect his official with a military escort.[2]

The Treasure Bearers
Ezra 8:24-30

Ezra set apart twelve priests and twelve Levites and placed the responsibility for the gold and silver in their hands. The phrase "Sherebiah, Hashabiah, and with them ten of their brothers" cannot be seen as identifying the twelve priests because Sherebiah and Hashabiah were Levites (cf. 8:18-19). As a result, we have two groups of twelve. The number twelve seems to have some significance for Ezra. He previously identified twelve different families in 8:3-14. Perhaps he consistently uses twelve to serve as a reminder of the twelve tribes of Israel. Evidently, the two heads of priestly families mentioned in 8:2 brought a number of their colleagues with them.

The treasure was weighed out to the group of treasure bearers. In the Pentateuch, the priests and Levites were given the responsibility of caring for the furnishings of the tabernacle (cf. Num. 3-4). Here they are essentially given the same responsibility with coins and utensils replacing the items of furniture. Ezra gives instructions that these treasure bearers are to "watch and keep" the treasure until they are able to present it to their brethren when the party reaches the temple in Jerusalem.

The amount of treasure is staggering. A Babylonian talent weighed close to 70 pounds. Therefore, the 650 silver and 100 gold talents together weighed almost 30 tons! Equally impressive are the various gold, silver, and bronze utensils. A Persian daric was a thick gold coin that weighed 130 grams (about 4 ½ ounces).

Ezra's Arrival in Jerusalem
Ezra 8:31-36

The company leaves the Ahava waterway on the twelfth of Nisan (late March, early April) of 458 B.C. They had originally planned to leave on the first day of the month; however, the need to recruit Levites delayed their start until the twelfth day (cf. 7:9). In effect, the trip had begun on the first day since that is when the exiles first left their homes and congregated on the banks of the Ahava waterway. The party sets out on their journey just two days before Passover.

The exiles have a safe journey and Ezra is again quick to give the Lord the credit with his customary phrase referring to the "hand" of God (cf. 7:6, 9, 28; 8:18, 22). The phrase "He delivered us from the hand of the enemy and the ambushes by the way" is somewhat misleading. At first glance it appears to be saying that the company was ambushed several times during their journey and the Lord delivered them in the midst of those ambushes. However, since the word translated "ambushes" is in the singular, the sentence is better translated "He saved us from enemy attack and from ambush on the way" (NEB). In other words, the Lord made sure that the exiles were never attacked during their journey.

The group arrives safely in Jerusalem on the first day of Ab (late August, early September) in 458 B.C. (7:9). The journey of almost a thousand miles is now complete. The pilgrims had traveled an average of about nine miles a day. Upon arrival in Jerusalem, the text notes that the exiles waited three days. Perhaps this was a time of rest following their rigorous journey. It is also possible that they arrived late in the week and waited until the Sabbath was over before weighing out the valuables, an activity that would have been considered work. On the fourth day, to celebrate their safe arrival in Jerusalem, the exiles offered the treasure to the priests and burnt offerings to the Lord. The valuables are weighed out to Meremoth son of Uriah. This same individual is mentioned in Nehemiah (cf. 3:4, 21). The burnt offerings expressed thanksgiving to the Lord and involved the whole-hearted consecration of the worshippers. The exiles also offered sin offerings. The sin offerings provided atonement for the sins of the worshippers.

After celebrating their arrival, the exiles deliver the king's edicts to his official representatives. The satraps and governors served as the king's administrators over the various provinces. During the time of Esther, the Persian Empire was comprised of 127 provinces, each governed by a satrap (cf. Es. 3:12). These satraps were primarily responsible for collecting the tribute owed to the king and for raising the armies needed to defend and expand the empire. Daniel 6:1 identifies the number of satraps appointed by Darius as being 120. The higher number of 127 is probably representative of the additional conquests made by the Persians since the time of Daniel. With more territory comes the need for more satraps. It is likely that the number continued to rise until present time. It is possible that there were now more than 130 satraps in the Persian Empire. The governors were subordinates of the satraps, responsible for small territories or even individual cities within a province. The provinces referred to here were located on the southwestern side of the Euphrates River ("beyond the River").

Study Questions
1. Do you think 7:28 should end chapter seven or begin chapter eight? Why?
2. What is the name of the waterway where Ezra camped?
3. Why does Ezra camp there?
4. Why do you think there were so few Levites who were willing to return?
5. How many people returned with Ezra?
6. Why do the people fast before their journey?

7. Who is given responsibility for the treasure? Why?
8. Why does Ezra refuse to ask the king for an armed escort?
9. Who is Meremoth?

Chapter 18
The Problem of Mixed Marriages
Ezra 9:1-4

Preview:
Ezra's mission was to apply the law in Israel. Through the law comes the knowledge of sin (Rom. 3:20). Such was the case in this passage.

The News of Apostasy (9:1-2)

At some point within a few months of the events of 8:33-36 (cf. 7:9; 10:9), the "princes" approach Ezra with news that many of the Jews were involved in mixed marriages with the foreigners[1] living in the land of Israel. The "princes" mentioned here are the leading men of the descendants of the Jewish remnant which had returned under Sheshbazzar. Evidently, these princes had done nothing to rectify the situation. However, at least some of them seem to view it as a problem since they are notifying Ezra of the situation. Many others were involved in the sin themselves (cf. 9:2b).

Since the meeting of elders described in 10:9 takes place four and a half months after Ezra's return, the question of Ezra's ignorance of this situation must be addressed. Surely he would have become aware of the problem if he had spent any amount of time among the people. The solution lies in the fact that Ezra evidently did not remain very long in the city of Jerusalem after his arrival. The final verse of chapter eight reveals that Ezra delivered the king's edicts to the "satraps" who were on the southwestern side of the Euphrates River ("beyond the River"). The plurality of the word "satraps" indicates that Ezra delivered these documents to satraps in several different provinces. This endeavor would naturally have taken several months, especially if the provinces in northern Africa are included. It is only upon his return from this mission that he learns of the apostasy of the Jews.

The list of foreigners is reminiscent of several similar lists in the Pentateuch (cf. Gen. 15:19-21; Ex. 23:23; 33:2; Deut. 20:17). The first group mentioned is the Canaanites. The Canaanites were the descendants of Canaan, the son of Ham. They are identified in Deuteronomy as one of the seven nations in the Promised Land "greater and stronger" than Israel (Deut. 7:1). The Canaanites lived along the eastern Mediterranean coastal regions from the River of Egypt to the area of Lebanon (Num. 13:29). The Canaanites, caught between the cumbersome writings of Mesopotamian cuneiform and Egyptian hieroglyphics, were the inventors of a simplified method of writing, the alphabet.[2] Biblical Hebrew is derived from the Canaanite language. The Canaanites were also known as artisans, bronze metallurgists, potters, and merchants. However, their most significant impact on Israel came in the area of religion. The Canaanite fertility cult was perhaps the most immoral and vile religion known to man. The chief god of the Canaanites was Baal, god of thunder and lightning. Other gods included El, the patriarchal deity who was the father of Baal; Yam, the god of the sea; Asherah, the wife of El; Mot, the god of the underworld; and Anat, the sister of Baal. The Canaanites worshipped their gods by engaging in sexual immorality involving male and female prostitutes and sacrificing their children. The Canaanite religion proved to be too attractive for the Hebrews to resist. Israel's worship of Baal seems to have been the most significant sin among those that led to the nation's deportation (cf. Jer. 11:17; Hos. 2:1-13; 11:2; Zeph. 1:4).

The second group mentioned is the Hittites. The Hittites were the descendants of Heth, the son of Canaan (Gen. 10:15). They are identified in Deuteronomy as one of the seven nations in the Promised Land "greater and stronger" than Israel (Deut. 7:1). Many scholars consider the Hittites as the third most influential people group of the Ancient Near East, rivaling the Egyptians and the Mesopotamians.[3] The Hittites dominated Asia Minor, their capital located on the Halys River at a place called Boghaz-keui in central Anatolia. Groups of Hittites migrated south, eventually settling in the hill country of Canaan near the city of Hebron (Gen. 23:19; Num. 13:29). Notable Hittites include Ephron, from whom Abraham purchased a burial site (Gen. 23), and Uriah, one of the mighty men of David (2 Sam. 23:39). Esau married two Hittites (Gen. 26:34) and Solomon had Hittite women in his harem (1 Kin. 11:1).

The third group mentioned is the Perizzites. The origin of the Perizzites is unknown. They first appear in Genesis 13:7 where they are simply identified as dwelling in the land of Canaan with the Canaanites at the time of Abraham (cf. Gen. 34:10). They are identified in Deuteronomy as one of the seven nations in the Promised Land "greater and stronger" than Israel (Deut. 7:1). During the period of the judges they lived in the heavily forested region near Mount Ephraim in the territory allotted to the tribes of Ephraim and West Manasseh (Judg. 17:15). The Perizzites may have lived in unwalled villages, probably located in the heavy forests mentioned above or in the low ground between hills (cf. the LXX rendering of Deut. 3:5; 1 Sam. 6:18).

The fourth group mentioned is the Jebusites. The Jebusites were the descendants of Canaan, the son of Ham (Gen. 10:16). They lived in the hill country (Num. 13:29) and were the original inhabitants of Jerusalem. Jebusite Jerusalem was taken by King David in about 1004 B.C. (cf. 2 Sam. 5:5-8). The Jebusites are identified in Deuteronomy as one of the seven nations in the Promised Land "greater and stronger" than Israel (Deut. 7:1). During the period of the judges they lived in the general region of Jerusalem in the territory allotted to the tribes of Judah and Benjamin (cf. Josh. 15:63; Judg. 1:21). It should be remembered that Jerusalem was among the cities allotted to the tribe of Benjamin (Josh. 18:28). Notable Jebusites include Adoni-zedek, the King of Jerusalem who formed the alliance against Gibeon (Josh. 10:1-4), and Araunah (also known as Ornan), from whom David bought the threshing floor which would become the site of Solomon's temple (2 Sam. 24:16-24; 1 Chr. 21:14-27). If Salem is identified as Jerusalem, then Melchizedek may have been a Jebusite (cf. Gen. 14:18).

The fifth group mentioned is the Ammonites. The Ammonites were the descendants of Ben-ammi, the son of an incestuous relationship between Lot and his younger daughter. The Ammonites lived on the eastern side of the Jordan River. The nation's territory was essentially surrounded by the Jabbok River and its tributaries. As a result, the border of Ammonite territory was referred to simply as the Jabbok River (Deut. 3:16; Josh. 12:2). The sources of the Jabbok River are near modern Amman, Jordan. This territory had previously belonged to the Rephaim, an ancient people who were displaced by the Ammonites (Deut. 2:20-21). The earliest documentation of hostilities between the Ammonites and the Children of Israel is the record of Judges 3:12-14, where the Ammonites join the coalition formed by Eglon, king of Moab. Jephthah later defeats an unnamed king of Ammon (Judg. 11). Notable Ammonites include Naamah, the wife of Solomon and mother of Rehoboam (1 Kin. 14:21, 31; 2 Chr. 12:13), and Tobiah, one of the major antagonists of Nehemiah (Neh. 2:19; 4:3). Solomon built a sanctuary for Molech, the "detestable" chief god of the Ammonites, on the Mount of Olives (1 Kin. 11:7). Child sacrifice was a significant part of the Ammonite Molech cult (Lev. 18:21; 20:2-5; 2 Kin. 23:10; Jer. 32:35).

The sixth group mentioned is the Moabites. The Moabites were the descendants of Moab, the son of an incestuous relationship between Lot and his older daughter. The Moabites lived on the eastern side of the Jordan River and the Dead Sea, just to the south of the Ammonites. The land of Moab was famous for its pasturage. 2 Kings 3:4 testifies to the agricultural wealth of the area, "Now Mesha king of Moab was a sheep breeder, and used to pay the king of Israel 100,000 lambs and the wool of 100,000 rams." The chief god of the Moabites was Chemosh (1 Kin. 11:7, 33). The worship of Chemosh included a priesthood (Jer. 48:7) and a sacrificial system (Num. 22:40; 25:2). The climate of Moab also allowed for the growing of wheat, barley, vineyards, and fruit trees.[4] Solomon married Moabite women and built a sanctuary for Chemosh on the Mount of Olives (1 Kin. 11:1, 7). Notable Moabites include the following: Balak, the king who hired Balaam to curse the Children of Israel (Num. 22-24); Eglon, the king who was assassinated by Ehud (Judg. 3:15-30); Ruth, the widow of Mahlon and wife of Boaz (Ruth 4:10, 13); and Mesha, the king who rebelled against King Jehoram of Israel (2 Kin. 3). Mesha is of special significance thanks to the archaeological discovery of the thirty-four-line Mesha Inscription, also known as the Moabite Stone. The Mesha Inscription dates to approximately 830 B.C. and commemorates Mesha's achievements, especially his overthrow of Omride oppression after the death of Omri. The text specifically names Omri king of Israel. It also specifically names Yahweh in the statement that Mesha, having captured an Israelite town, "took from there the vessels of Yahweh and dragged them before Chemosh" (lines 17-18).

The seventh group mentioned is the Egyptians. The land of Egypt is strategically located at the northeastern tip of Africa, forming a land bridge to the continent of Asia. The most significant feature of the land of Egypt is the Nile River. In fact, Egypt is often called "the gift of the Nile." Because the Nile River flows from south to north, southern Egypt is known as Upper Egypt while northern Egypt is known as Lower Egypt. The Egyptians may be the descendants of Ham, the son of Noah. The land of Egypt is sometimes identified as the land of Ham in the Old Testament (Ps. 78:51; 105:23, 27; 106:22). Like Israel, Egypt was a land of religion. Herodotus notes, "They [the Egyptians] are beyond measure religious, more than any other nation. . . . Their religious observances are, one might say, innumerable" (*Histories* 2.37). The chief god of the Egyptians was Ra, the sun god. However, many other gods were routinely worshipped including Osiris, god of the Nile, and Isis, goddess of children. These gods were shown to be inferior to Yahweh through the ten plagues sent upon Egypt, thus demonstrating that the God of Israel is the most powerful Being in the universe. While the various gods were certainly important to the Egyptians, the single most significant ingredient of Egyptian religion was the pharaoh. Hoffmeier explains,

> The Egyptian pharaohs were viewed as divine and were associated with Horus. The foundation for this belief was rooted in the myth of Osiris, Horus, and Seth, which is known from the Old Kingdom Pyramid Texts, the later Coffin texts, and the Memphite Theology. Because of this mythic foundation, the pharaoh was always the focal point of

Egyptian religion, the ultimate high priest who built temples and oversaw their maintenance.[5] These massive temples, including those at Karnak and Luxor, were reserved for the priesthood and were usually off limits to the laity. Notable Egyptians include Shishak, the pharaoh who invaded Israel during the reign of Rehoboam (1 Kin. 14:25-26), and Neco, the pharaoh of the army who met Josiah in battle at Megiddo, a battle in which Josiah was fatally shot by the Egyptian archers (2 Kin. 23:29; 2 Chr. 35:22-23).

The eighth and final group mentioned is the Amorites. The name Amorites is derived from the Akkadian *Amurru*, meaning "west." They were the descendants of Canaan, the son of Ham (Gen. 10:16). The Amorites lived to the west of Mesopotamia and thus were called "westerners." The Amorites had their origins in Syria and migrated south into the land of Canaan. They were so numerous that the land of Canaan is called *Amurri* in the Amarna letters. The Amorites are identified in Deuteronomy as one of the seven nations in the Promised Land "greater and stronger" than Israel (Deut. 7:1). The Amorites lived in the hill country on both sides of the Jordan River (Num. 13:29; Josh. 5:1). The so-called King's Highway traversed their territory (Num. 21:21-22). They were largely nomadic shepherds, supplying sheep and goats to the Canaanite cities. Notable Amorites include Sihon and Og, two Kings who were defeated by the Israelites on their way to the promised land (Num. 21).

Deuteronomy 7:1-4 is a passage which relates directly to Ezra 9:1-2. The various people groups mentioned in both passages are the Hittites, Amorites, Canaanites, Perizzites, and Jebusites. The command of Deuteronomy 7:1 is specifically addressed against the nations which at that time occupied the land of Israel. Since the current situation involved other foreign groups living in the land of Israel, Ezra is correct in broadening the scope of the original command to include these other nations as well. Deuteronomy 7:2-3 explicitly forbids any relationship with these nations, "you shall make no covenant with them and show no favor to them. Furthermore, you shall not intermarry with them; you shall not give your daughters to their sons, nor shall you take their daughters for your sons." The reason given by the Lord; "For they will turn your sons away from following Me to serve other gods; then the anger of the Lord will be kindled against you, and He will quickly destroy you" (Deut. 7:4). The nation had originally been sent into exile for precisely this reason. They could be removed from their land yet again.

The Lord's prohibition had nothing to do with a hatred for foreign peoples. The command was designed to keep the worship of Israel pure. Fensham elaborates,

The reason for this attitude had nothing to do with racism, but with a concern for the purity of the religion of the Lord. Marriages with foreigners, especially when those foreigners were in an important position as in the time of Ezra, were fraught with problems for the Jews. The influence of a foreign mother, with her connection to another religion, on her children would ruin the pure religion of the Lord and would create a syncretistic religion running contrary to everything in the Jewish faith. In the end it was a question of the preservation of their identity, their religious identity.[6]

This fact is also evidenced in the use of the phrase "holy race."[7] This phrase is an obvious allusion to the phrase "holy people" used throughout Deuteronomy in reference to the Children of Israel (cf. 7:6 14:2, 21; 28:9). Even today, many Jewish leaders regard intermarriage as the most serious threat to their religion. Marmur writes, "the greatest danger to Jewish survival outside Israel today is not anti-Semitism

but assimilation, epitomized by the threat of intermarriage .
. . [intermarriage] is a direct threat to Judaism, for without
Jews Judaism cannot exist."[8]

Ezra's Reaction (9:3-4)

Ezra is understandably appalled by the tragic news. He
tears his clothes, pulls out some of his hair, and collapses on
the ground. Ezra's behavior upon learning of sin among the
remnant is a marked contrast from that of Nehemiah; "So I
contended with them and cursed them and struck some of
them and pulled out their hair, and made them swear by God,
'You shall not give your daughters to their sons, nor take
of their daughters for your sons or for yourselves'" (Neh.
13:25). Ezra the priest pulls out his own hair while Nehemiah
the governor pulls out the hair of the offenders.

Ezra sits down in a public place where the nation could
see his grief. The reference to the evening sacrifices indicates
that he probably sat near the temple (cf. 9:5; 10:6). Ezra is
quickly joined by those who realized that the remnant was
in danger of suffering the judgment of God. The Lord had
issued a stern warning to His people almost a thousand years
earlier. If the nation intermarries with foreigners, "then the
anger of the Lord will be kindled against you, and He will
quickly destroy you" (Deut. 7:4). The remnant obviously
sees this warning given to their ancestors as still applicable
to them in their current age. The "exiles" in this passage is a
reference to the descendants of those Jews who had returned
under Sheshbazzar and were living in Judah prior to Ezra's
return. Ezra remains in a state of mourning until the time of
the evening sacrifices (about 3:00 pm).

Study Questions
1. Why is Ezra unaware of the problem of mixed
   marriages?

2. Why was the Canaanite religion so attractive to the Jews?
3. Who was the chief god of the Canaanites?
4. Who were the original inhabitants of Jerusalem?
5. Who was the chief god of the Ammonites?
6. Who was the chief god of the Moabites?
7. Why were the Jews forbidden from marrying foreign women?
8. What does Ezra do when he learns of the sin of the remnant?

Chapter 19
The Prayer of Ezra
Ezra 9:5-15

---⊗⊗⊗---

Preview:

Both Ezra and Nehemiah are men of prayer. This is the most significant prayer of Ezra recorded in this book. As you read through this prayer by Ezra, pay attention to the structure of the prayer and look for ways to incorporate the methods used by Ezra into your own prayers.

The Time of the Prayer (9:5)

At about 3:00 pm, when it was time for the evening sacrifices to be offered to the Lord by the priests, Ezra rose from his "humiliation." The word "humiliation" is a reference to his state of sitting in a public place while mourning with torn garments (cf. 9:3). Soon after rising, Ezra falls on his knees and stretches out his hands to the Lord. Solomon assumed this same position when he offered up his prayer of dedication for the temple (cf. 1 Kin. 8:54; 2 Chr. 6:13). The act of kneeling during prayer was evidently common (cf. Dan. 6:10; perhaps also 1 Kin. 18:42), as was spreading out one's hands (cf. Ps. 88:9; Isa. 1:15; perhaps also Lam. 1:17, figuratively speaking). The practice of kneeling probably grew out of the tradition of subjects kneeling before their kings. Stretching out one's hands may represent a gesture of need.[1] The acts of kneeling and raising hands to the Lord during prayer are repeated in the New Testament (cf. Acts 7:60; Eph. 3:14; 1 Tim. 2:8).

The Sins of the Nation (9:6-7)

Ezra begins his prayer with a statement of humiliation. Ezra is humiliated because of the sins of his people. Confession of sin is the major theme of this prayer. Ezra's feelings of solidarity with his people come through in his use of the first person throughout this prayer. Even though he had not personally committed the specific sin he is praying about, he still identifies himself with the remnant as a whole (e.g., "our iniquities," "our guilt"). In this respect, he is reminiscent of the Servant in Isaiah 53:12 who was "numbered with the transgressors" and "interceded for the transgressors."

The phrases "our iniquities have risen above our heads" and "our guilt has grown even to the heavens" are an example of synonymous parallelism commonly found in Hebrew poetry. The two lines are identical in their meaning. The great sins of past generations are being added to by the current generation. They had not learned from the judgment of their ancestors. They were committing the same sins as their forefathers. Ezra realizes that the exile of the Jews happened as a result of their sin. Therefore, the current generation could receive the same punishment. The phrase "kings of the lands" is a reference to the kings of Assyria and Babylon who were used by the Lord to exile His people. The major theme of the passage is the judgment of the Jews that resulted in exile (cf. "given into the hand," "captivity"). This is because Ezra is naturally worried that his current generation might be judged in the same way.

The Faithfulness of God (9:8-9)

Even though the nation had proved unfaithful to Him, the Lord still proved faithful to His covenants. He had chosen to show mercy to His people for a "brief moment" by leaving an "escaped remnant." The "brief moment" spoken of by Ezra is a reference to the eighty years since the decree of Cyrus allowing the Jews to return to their land. This decree had been issued in 538 B.C. Ezra's return takes place in 458 B.C. The nation is still in their land. It can be assumed that there was a somewhat steady migration of Jews back to Israel throughout these eighty years, including the returns of Sheshbazzar and Ezra. The Jews of these various returns are the "escaped remnant." They had escaped from their exile. The nation, however, had suffered tremendously as a result of the exiles. Their population had been decimated. The decimation of the Jewish population is seen in the repetition of the term "remnant" in this prayer (8, 13, 14, 15). Perhaps a few hundred thousand Jews lived in Israel during the time of Ezra. Millions had been killed or carried away into captivity by the Assyrians and Babylonians.

Ezra again uses Hebrew synonymous parallelism as he illustrates the phrase "escaped remnant" by calling them a "peg in His holy place." The phrase "holy place" is a reference to the land of Judah as a whole, and perhaps Jerusalem in particular. The word "peg" literally means "tent peg" or "stake." The word has its roots in nomadic life and refers to a place reached after a long journey where a tent is pitched.[2] The word is used figuratively in this passage and refers to the foothold achieved with the initial returns on the part of the remnant. Just as the erecting of a tent begins with a stake driven into the ground, so the rebuilding of the nation of

Israel is seen to begin with the "escaped remnant" serving as the initial foothold.

The result of this foothold is twofold. First, the return to the land "enlightens" the "eyes" of the nation. This phrase literally refers to the immediate sense of physical revival which nourishment can bring following a period of hunger and thirst.[3] This idea is vividly demonstrated in the account of Jonathan in 1 Samuel 14 where this same phrase occurs two times. In this passage, Jonathan unwittingly broke his father's command against eating food when he ate some honey after a long day of battle. Immediately after eating the honey, Jonathan had his "eyes brightened" (v. 27). He later adds, "See now, how my eyes have brightened because I tasted a little of this honey" (v. 29). In the same way, the initial returns gave the nation of Israel an immediate sense of physical revival. Second, the return to the land served to demonstrate a "little reviving" in the midst of the nation's bondage. The author evidently considered the nation dead during the exile and in need of revival (cf. Ezek. 37:1-14). Although the nation was still subservient to a foreign power, the various returns were the initial signs of the resurrection of Israel.

Ezra next goes into more detail concerning his reference to the nation's bondage. He maintains that the Jews are still in slavery, that is, subservient to another nation. However, in the midst of this slavery, the Lord had not forsaken His people. He had extended "lovingkindness" (Hebrew *hesed*; "loyal covenant love;" see the note on 3:11) to the nation by raising up the Persians. The reference to the Persian kings should be seen in opposition to the "kings of the lands" in verse seven. The "kings of the lands" (i.e. Assyria, Babylon) were the kings used by God to judge His people. The Persian kings were and are being used by God as His instrument of deliverance for the Jews (Isa. 45:1-7). God raised up these Persian kings and stirred their hearts to allow the remnant to return to the land of Israel, to restore the temple of Yahweh, and to rebuild the walls of the city of Jerusalem.

The phrase "give us a wall in Judah and Jerusalem" has been used by scholars to argue that Ezra returned after Nehemiah. However, Ezra 4:12 clearly describes the work of Ezra and the remnant to rebuild the walls of the city. It can be assumed that Ezra was doing this project with the initial permission of King Artaxerxes (cf. 7:6). At the time of the prayer recorded in these verses, Ezra is fully anticipating the rebuilding of the walls of Jerusalem. It is not until Artaxerxes issues his response to Rehum that the work of rebuilding the walls of the city is halted (cf. 4:23). Williamson, holding to a metaphorical interpretation of the phrase, offers another view,

A metaphorical interpretation is by no means impossible in the present context, where several of the phrases have already been seen to fall into this pattern, and indeed two considerations make it more probable. First, the qualifying phrase "in Judah and Jerusalem" would be very odd if the reference were merely to the city wall. Second, the word used here is not at all the normal word for a city wall. It usually refers to a wall or fence around a vineyard or along a road. Only in one other passage could it even possibly mean "city wall" (Mic. 7:11), and even there it is not completely certain that this is what is meant. In any event, the writer was more concerned in a prophecy of restoration, to use a term that refers to the enclosure of a vineyard, a traditional metaphor for Israel in their enjoyment of a healthy relationship with Yahweh.[4]

The Words of the Prophets (9:10-12)

Instead of requesting the Lord's mercy, Ezra admits the failure of his people. He acknowledges that they have forsaken the commandments of the Lord that had been revealed through His prophets. These verses are a rather obvious allusion to the teachings of Moses in Deuteronomy 7:1-3. The plurality of the word "prophets" reveals that this topic was also a common theme in prophetic sermons (cf. Mal. 2:11). Moses and the other prophets had instructed the nation to refrain from intermarrying with the peoples of the land. This command was given in hopes of maintaining the purity of Israel. The foreigners were unclean and a union with them would make the Jews unclean. If a clean towel is united with a dirty towel then the dirty towel makes the clean towel dirty; the clean towel does not make the dirty towel clean. So it was with the people of God and the foreigners in the land.

The Future of the Remnant (9:13-15)

Even though the lord had severely punished the Jews, He had not completely destroyed them. Ezra acknowledges that the Lord had every right to destroy His people and credits Him with showing mercy. The Lord had left a remnant, a group of Jews who were able to escape the judgment of the Lord by returning from exile. Now this remnant was in danger of repeating the sins of their ancestors. Ezra realizes that the repetition of this great sin would endanger the very life of the nation. God might completely destroy His people this time just as He had threatened to do with the generation that bowed before the golden calf (Ex. 32:10).

Ezra closes his prayer with another statement of confession before the Lord. The word translated "righteous" is better translated "gracious" or "merciful." In other words, the Lord has been merciful to the Jews by leaving an escaped remnant instead of utterly destroying His people. Ezra, realizing the possibility of God's judgment, acknowledges the mercy of God and once again admits the failure of his people. The sins of the few became the responsibility of the whole, with the result that no one was able to "stand," i.e., be regarded as guiltless, before the Lord. A little leaven had leavened the whole lump (cf. 1 Cor. 5:6). It was now Ezra's job to "clean out the old leaven" (1 Cor. 5:7) by taking steps to purify the remnant.

Study Questions
1. At what time does Ezra pray?
2. Why do you think he chose this time?
3. Why does Ezra use the first person when he refers to the sins of the nation?
4. How long is the "brief moment?"
5. What does the phrase "peg in His holy place" refer to?
6. Why did God raise up the Persians?
7. What did you learn about prayer from analyzing the prayer of Ezra?

Chapter 20
The Solution to the Problem
Ezra 10:1-8

—◦◦◦—

Preview:
Ezra's leadership technique in this book largely involved leadership by spiritual example. In this passage, you can see how effective this style of leadership can be. Not all leaders have to be aggressive with the people placed under their care. Allow the Holy Spirit's conviction to work in your favor.

The Approach of the People (10:1)

While Ezra was praying the prayer of 9:6-15, a sizable portion of the Jewish remnant gathered to him. The crowd was made up of men, women, and children. These people were not curious onlookers; they were convicted by Ezra's spiritual mourning and wept bitterly. The reference to children "introduces a note of tragic gravity as it reminds the reader of the possible social consequences of the proceedings about to be initiated, a point recapitulated in the last verse of the chapter."[1] Unlike Nehemiah (cf. Neh. 13:8, 11, 15, 17, 25, 28), Ezra did not need to forcefully rebuke the nation. His actions spoke louder than words.

It should be noted at the outset that Ezra returns to writing in the third person in this chapter to describe his activities (cf. e.g., 7:6-10). Throughout chapter nine, Ezra had consistently written in the first person (9:1, 3, 4, 5, 6). This fact has been used by many scholars to accept a different source for chapter 10, claiming that it could not have been written by Ezra. Ezra is writing in the third person to emphasize the repentance of the nation.[2]

The Recommendation of Shecaniah (10:2-4)

Shecaniah speaks on behalf of the remnant. Shecaniah is identified as the son of Jehiel, one of the sons of Elam. There are several other Shecaniahs mentioned in Ezra and Nehemiah (cf. Ezra 8:3, 5; Neh. 3:29; 6:18; 12:3). It is difficult to identify this Shecaniah with any of them. The length of Shecaniah's genealogy indicates that he was a person of some importance, certainly to be identified among the leading men of the remnant (cf. 9:1). The family of Elam had returned to Jerusalem from Babylon with Zerubbabel and Jeshua (cf. 2:2, 7). The family of Elam is also mentioned in 8:7, and 10:26, indicating that it was one of the most significant families in the postexilic community.

Shecaniah begins his speech to Ezra by confessing the sins of the people. He admits to the fact that the remnant was being unfaithful to Yahweh by marrying foreign women. Note that Shecaniah uses the first person plural much like Ezra did in his prayer of 9:6-15. Since Shecaniah is not listed among those who were guilty of this sin (cf. 10:18-44), it can be assumed that he was simply another faithful Jew like Ezra who had a heart filled with concern for the spiritual welfare of his people. If the Jehiel of 10:26 is to be identified with the father of Shecaniah, then Shecaniah's own family was involved in this sin. Even though the nation has sinned against God, hope is not lost. The nation can repent of their behavior and take steps to remove their offense. Shecaniah realizes that God might refrain from judging the nation if they repent and change their ways (cf. Joel 2:12-14; Jon. 3:9-10). Shecaniah recommends that the remnant make a covenant with God to "put away" all the foreign wives and their children. Shecaniah's recommendation advocates divorce, not separation. The word translated "put away" is the same word used in Deuteronomy 24:2 ("leaves") in the context of divorce. Fensham explains,

> Foreign women were married contrary to the law of God. The marriages were illegal from the outset. The sending away of the women is to guard the exiles against the continuation of an illegal act. With their foreign wives they lived in sin. It is thus clear from v. 4 that there is a strong legal background against which Shecaniah has formulated his proposal. The dividing line between the permissible and impermissible is strongly emphasized.[3]

In the Ancient Near East mothers received custody of the children when they were divorced (cf. Gen. 21:14). In effect, the Jewish men were divorcing both their foreign wives and the offspring created by their unholy union. Fensham elaborates,

> Even the children born from the illegal marriages must be sent away. This proposal is harsh in the light of modern Christian conceptions. Why should innocent children be punished? We must remember that the religious influence of the mothers on their children was regarded as the stumbling block. To keep the religion of the Lord pure was the one and only aim of Ezra and the returned exiles. As a small minority group, the repatriates lived in the Holy Land among

a large population of influential people who were followers of various polytheistic religions. Against such larger numbers they had to defend themselves and their religious identity. Thus the drastic measures are understandable.[4]

These marriages were viewed as sinful in the eyes of God. Nehemiah writes, "You have committed all this great evil by acting unfaithfully against our God by marrying foreign women" (Neh. 13:27).

The phrase "according to the law" probably refers to the law recorded in Deuteronomy 24:1-4 which provides specific procedures for divorce. According to this passage, the husband is allowed to divorce his wife if he finds "some indecency" in her (24:1). Having been influenced by the preaching of Ezra, the remnant now finds something indecent about being married to foreign women. The passage also requires that the husband provide the wife with a "certificate of divorce" at the time of the divorce (24:1). This certificate renounced the husband's rights to his wife and she was then able to get remarried.

The proposal of Shecaniah is reminiscent of the actions taken by the Jews in Joshua's day. After a somewhat successful campaign to conquer the land of Canaan, the nation congregated at Shechem to make a covenant with the Lord. In that covenant, the nation resolved to put away their foreign gods and serve only the Lord (Josh. 24:23-25). Unfortunately, both covenants, Ezra's and Joshua's, would prove to be short-lived.

Shecaniah ends his speech by informing Ezra that the spiritual condition of the nation is his responsibility. He calls on Ezra to take steps to rectify the problem, promising the scribe that the people will be behind him. The urgency of Shecaniah's plea is reflected in the force of the imperatives. He calls on Ezra to "arise!," "be courageous!," and "act!" Here we again see the difference in personality between Ezra and Nehemiah. It is evident from Nehemiah 13 (cf. 8, 25, 28) that the governor never needed anyone's encouragement to act forcefully.

The Proclamation to Assemble in Jerusalem (10:5-8)

Upon hearing the words of Shecaniah, Ezra rose from his knees. He made the elders of the Jews take an oath that they would follow the advice of Shecaniah. Once again, the Jews are divided into three groups, i.e., the priests, the Levites, and the laity (cf. 9:1). Oath taking was customary in the Ancient Near East (cf. Josh. 6:26; Jud. 21:5; Neh. 6:18).

Ezra next goes to the chamber of Jehohanan. This chamber would have been one of the many rooms in the temple (cf. 8:29). Jehohanan is identified as the son of Eliashib. It is possible that this Eliashib is the same Eliashib who was high priest in the days of Nehemiah (cf. Neh. 3:1; 20). Nehemiah 13:4 indicates that an Eliashib was in charge of these chambers in Nehemiah's day. If this Eliashib is not the high priest, then it is also possible that this is the Eliashib mentioned here in Ezra. It is unknown why Ezra went to this chamber. Perhaps he wanted to enlist the support of Jehohanan. It is also possible that he wanted to confer with one of the religious leaders of the remnant before progressing with his plan.

While at the chamber of Jehohanan, Ezra continues mourning over the sins of his people. The text notes that Ezra is in the midst of fasting. At this point, Ezra has torn his garments, pulled out his hair and beard, sat down, fallen on his knees, stretched out his hands, prayed, made confession, wept, prostrated himself, taken an oath, and fasted (cf. 9:3, 5; 10:1, 5, 6). Ezra's behavior reveals not only his love for his people, but also his hatred for sin. It should be remembered that Ezra has not even personally committed the sin over which he is in such extreme anguish. May our response be the same when we view sin in our midst today.

Together, Ezra, Jehohanan, and the leaders of the remnant make a proclamation calling on the exiles to assemble in Jerusalem. The proclamation allowed the exiles three days to make their way to Jerusalem. Judah was a very small territory at this time and Jerusalem could easily be reached within three days from any city in the region. The proclamation included a promise of harsh judgment on all those who were unwilling to come; their property will be "forfeited" and they will be excluded from the community. The word translated "forfeited" (Hebrew *haram*) originally meant "utterly destroy." Throughout the early years of Israel's history it was used to denote the complete and utter annihilation of a person or thing (cf. Deut. 2:34; Josh. 6:21; 10:28; 1 Sam. 15:3). By the time of the exile, the word has lost its force and takes on the meaning of "confiscate," or "devote" (cf. Ezek 44:29), as it is used in this passage. While the confiscation of one's property was bad enough, it was nothing compared to being shunned by the community. Fensham elaborates,

> The culprits will be removed from the community, viz., they would not be allowed at the service of the temple, and it might also mean that they would forfeit their rights as citizens. These were for Jews severe measures indeed. They were then not allowed to partake in the daily sacrifices for the removing of their sins. They were totally cut off from other members of the community and could expect no help in times of distress. They were regarded as foreigners without any claim on the religious communion of the exiles.[5]

The authority given to Ezra by King Artaxerxes allowed him the opportunity to make this threat (cf. 7:26). The warning had the full backing of the Persian government.

1167993

VOTER REGISTRATION CERTIFICATE
(Certificado de Registro Electoral)

HARRIS COUNTY (Condado)

VUID (NUID)	Gender (Sexo)	Valid from (Válido desde)
1104948474	M	01/01/08

Year of Birth (Año de Nacimiento)	Prec. No. (Pct. Núm.)	thru (hasta)
1986	0119	12/31/09

Name and Permanent Residence Address (Nombre y dirección residencial permanente)

NATHAN ALLAN COTTON
3238 GOLDEN EYE
KATY TX 77493

X

VOTER MUST PERSONALLY SIGN HIS/HER NAME IMMEDIATELY UPON RECEIPT, IF ABLE
(El votante debe firmar esta tarjeta personalmente al punto de recibirla, si puede.)

Voted in the _____ Party Primary
(Votó en la elección primaria del partido político nombrado arriba)

Cert. No. (Núm. de Cert.) 58654567

U.S. REP. (Rep. Federal)	STATE SEN. (Sen. Estatal)	STATE REP. (Rep. Estatal)	COMM. PREC. (Com. Pcto.)	JUSTICE PREC. (Just. Pcto.)	SCHOOL (Escuela)	CITY (Ciudad)
10	07	132	3	05	019	063

Name and Mailing Address (Nombre y dirección de correo)

*****AUTO**SCH 5-DIGIT 77493
NATHAN ALLAN COTTON
3238 GOLDEN EYE
KATY TX 77493-4866

You may vote without your certificate by showing another form of identification. **If you lose your certificate, you may request a replacement certificate by contacting the voter registrar.** (Usted podrá votar sin su certificado de votante si presenta otra forma de identificación. Si pierde su certificado, usted podrá pedir un certificado de reemplazo comunicándose con el registrador de votantes.)

If you registered to vote by mail, and you have never voted in a federal election in Texas, you must present a form of identification in addition to your voter registration certificate. Call one of the numbers on the reverse of this card for information about acceptable forms of identification. (Si se registró para votar por correo y nunca ha votado en una elección federal dentro de Texas, debe presentar otra forma de identificación además de su certificado de votante. Favor de llamar uno de los números en el reverso de esta tarjeta para información sobre las formas de identificación aceptables.)

You will receive a new certificate every two years as long as your voter registration is not cancelled under some provision of the law. Voting by use of this certificate by any person other than the person in whose name this certificate is issued is a felony. (Usted recibirá un certificado nuevo cada dos años mientras que no se cancele su registración bajo alguna disposición de la ley. El uso de este certificado para votar por alguna persona que no sea la persona cuyo nombre aparece en el certificado es un delito grave.)

If you move within the county, you must transfer your registration to your new precinct. You may vote a full ballot at your previous precinct if your registration has not become effective in your new precinct. Before you are allowed to vote in the previous precinct, the election judge will ask you to fill out a statement of residence confirming your new address in your new precinct. (Si usted cambia de domicilio dentro del mismo condado, deberá transferir su inscripción de votante después del cambio. En caso de que no haya entrado en vigencia su inscripción en el nuevo precinto, podrá votar con boleta íntegra en su precinto anterior. Antes de darle autorización para votar en el precinto anterior, el juez electoral le pedirá que llene una declaración de residencia para confirmar su nueva dirección en el precinto nuevo.)

If you move from one Texas county to another, you must re-register in the county of your new residence. You may be eligible to vote a limited ballot after you move if your new registration is not yet effective and you were registered to vote in your previous county of residence when you moved. Contact the county clerk or elections administrator in your new county for information. (Si usted se cambia de residencia de un condado a otro dentro del Estado de Texas, usted deberá registrarse de nuevo en el condado de su residencia nueva. Usted puede tener derecho a votar una boleta limitada después de cambiar su residencia si su nuevo certificado de votante todavía no está vigente y si usted es uvo registrado para votar en su residencia previa de condado cuando se mudo. Para recibir información, comuníquese con el Secretario del Condado o el administrador de elecciones del condado de su residencia nueva.)

If any information on this certificate changes or is incorrect, correct the information in the space provided below, sign and return this certificate to the voter registrar. (Si resulta que alguna información en este certificado de votante cambia o está incorrecta, favor de corregir la información en el espacio provisto abajo, y luego firme y devuelva este certificado de votante al registrador de votantes.)

Cần giúp đỡ bằng tiếng Việt hãy gọi số 713-368-2202.

I affirm the changes made to the left are correct. (Afirmo que los cambios hechos al lado izquierdo están correctos.)

X _____

Study Questions
1. What is the effect of Ezra's spiritual mourning?
2. Who is Shecaniah?
3. What is the recommendation of Shecaniah?
4. What is your opinion of Ezra's leadership style?
5. Who is Jehohanan?
6. What are some of the forms of mourning that Ezra participates in?

Chapter 21
The Assembly in Jerusalem
Ezra 10:9-44

Preview:

How would you like the fact that you had committed a great sin against the Lord preserved for all eternity? Imagine the shame felt by each Jew whose name was put on the list recorded in this chapter. One would think that the Jews would learn from their mistakes and stop messing around with foreign women!

Ezra's Call for Repentance (10:9-11)

The exiles respond positively to the decree of the Jewish leaders and assemble in Jerusalem three days after the proclamation was delivered. The reference here to Judah and Benjamin is probably a geographical notation as opposed to a tribal indication. The assembly took place on the twentieth day of the ninth month (i.e., Chislev; late November and early December), 458 B.C. The exiles congregate in the open square in front of the temple. This square could accommodate thousands of people[1] and was probably the only place in the city large enough to hold this gathering. It should be remembered that most of the city still lay in ruins (cf. Neh. 1:3). Another reason the congregation met within close proximity of the temple was because of the religious nature of the occasion. Surely many of the Jews would have wanted to offer sacrifices when confronted with their sin (cf. 10:19).

The text notes that the exiles sitting in the open square of the temple were trembling. Two reasons for this phenomenon are provided. First, the exiles were trembling because of the sheer magnitude of this matter. Clearly, they understood the significance of the occasion. Many of their lives were about to be forever changed. Many were going to lose wives and children. Perhaps even many feared for their lives, knowing that Ezra had the authority to put them to death (cf. 7:26). Second, the remnant was trembling because of the heavy rains. These rains would not only have been extremely heavy, but also bitterly cold. The crowd was thus experiencing both an internal emotional anxiety and an external physical distress.

As the masses huddle under the driving rain, Ezra rose to speak to the assembly. His speech was short but powerful. It is comprised of four key elements. First, the scribe accused the exiles of being unfaithful to the Lord by marrying foreign women. Second, Ezra explained that their personal sin had communal implications, it added to the guilt of the nation. The entire nation could be exiled as a result of the sins of a few. Third, the scribe called on the people to "make confession" to the Lord. The phrase "make confession" is literally "give thanksgiving." It was probably a popular idiom for expressing heartfelt repentance. Before a person can truly thank the Lord, he must first repent and make confession. Therefore, the idiom used here refers to the whole process.

Fourth and finally, Ezra commanded the remnant to do the will of God, namely, to separate from foreigners, especially the foreign wives.

These verses make it difficult, if not impossible, to hold to the view that God does not permit divorce for any reason. It is obvious in this passage that Ezra is following the law very carefully. He is a scribe "skilled in the law of Moses" (7:6). Furthermore, he is writing (and acting) under the inspiration of the Spirit. In this passage, Ezra not only permits divorce, he forcefully commands that the procedure take place. Perhaps most importantly, he claims that this separation is the very will of God. "By this action the community was not saying that divorce was good. It was a matter of following God's Law about the need for religious purity in the nation (Ex. 34:11-16; Deut. 7:1-4)."[2]

Since these verses reveal that it was God's will for these divorces to take place, this passage must be reconciled with the words of Ezra's contemporary, the prophet Malachi. In Malachi 2:16 the prophet condemns divorce, even emphasizing the fact that God hates divorce. However, this statement by Malachi must be understood in its context. The divorces that God hates are those in which His people "deal treacherously" (Mal. 2:16). From the context, it is clear that the individuals with whom the Jews have "dealt treacherously" are the wives of their "youth" (Mal. 2:14; see also 2:15). The phrase "your youth" indicates that these Jews had previously been married. The wives of their youth are not the wives with whom they are currently living. The wives of their youth were Jewish wives with whom the Jews had made a "covenant" while God served as a "witness," thereby indicating that He approved of this relationship (2:14). In other words, these Jews had divorced their Jewish wives to marry foreign wives. Malachi calls these second marriages "an abomination" and asserts that those guilty have "profaned the sanctuary of the Lord" (Mal. 2:11). One can assume from the passage that the prophet is calling on his audience to divorce their current foreign wives and return to the wives of their youth, that is, their Jewish wives. The reason given is because God hated that original divorce. Viewed in this way, the prophet Malachi is preaching the same message as that of Ezra, namely, that God hates intermarriage between His people and unbelieving foreigners. One must assume that foreign believers were considered acceptable marriage material in the sight of God (e.g., Rahab, Ruth). This was God's will for His people in the Old Testament. It is inappropriate to command modern believers to divorce their unbelieving spouses (cf. 1 Cor. 7:12-14).

The Response of the Assembly (10:12-15)

The assembly responds favorably to the speech of Ezra. They cry out their approval with a loud voice. They recognize that it is their duty to follow the commands of God. The words of the congregation as a whole end with the close of verse twelve. It is likely that the words of verses thirteen and fourteen were spoken by a few representatives who realized the enormous challenges in undertaking this endeavor.

The representatives supply two reasons why the congregation cannot immediately follow the command of Ezra. First, the sheer volume of people involved in this sin meant that a certain amount of time was required to organize and investigate their cases. Second, the weather prevented immediate action. It was the middle of the winter rainy season and the exiles were forces to stand in the open. These conditions made a thorough investigation impractical at the present time. The reasons provided by the representatives should not be viewed as a way of circumventing the problem since they offer a solution in the very next verse.

The representatives suggest that the leaders represent the congregation. These leaders would be responsible for identifying the men in their community who had committed the sin of intermarriage. At appointed times these leaders would come to Jerusalem with the guilty parties for an investigative hearing. The presence of local leaders helped to ensure that the hearings were fair and balanced.

The proposal of the representatives ends with the phrase "until the fierce anger of our God on account of this matter is turned away from us." At this point, the anger of God has only been mentioned as a possible threat in Ezra's prayer (9:14). Nowhere is there any mention of God withholding blessings for this generation of exiles such as was the case in Haggai's day when the remnant stopped working on the temple (Hag. 1:6-11). If God's anger had already been shown to the people, then the scribe for some reason chose not to reveal it in his narrative. Perhaps he wanted to picture the congregation's repentance as being motivated by religious fervor rather than as an attempt to regain the favor of God, i.e., material blessings.

The congregation was almost unanimous in its agreement. Only Jonathan and Jahzeiah, supported by Meshullam and Shabbethai (Neh. 8:7; 11:16) are in opposition to the agreement. The question is, to what were they opposed; the decision to divorce the foreign women or the decision to take some time to carry out the decree? It would be unusual, though certainly not impossible, for the modifying exception clause "only . . . opposed this" (10:15) to occur so far after the original statement "all the assembly" (10:12). As a result, the second option is to be preferred. These four individuals should be seen as wanting to resolve the matter as quickly as possible. They evidently regarded the delay to be unnecessary.

The Meshullam mentioned here may have been the Meshullam who returned with Ezra (8:16). The connection is not certain since Meshullam was an extremely common name at this time (cf. Neh. 3:4, 6; 6:18; 8:4; 10:7, 20; 11:7, 11; 12:13, 16, 25). Since Meshullam is mentioned in 10:29

as one of those guilty of intermarriage, it is possible that he was unwilling to divorce his wife, lending credence to the view that he was opposed to the decision to divorce. However, it is equally possible that since he was directly involved, he wanted to resolve the situation as quickly as possible, as noted above. The others do not appear in the list. Nothing further is known of Jonathan and Jahzeiah. Shabbethai is identified in Nehemiah 8:7 and 11:16 as being a leader among the Levites.

The Investigation Hearings (10:16-17)

Ezra selected leaders from each family who were responsible for identifying those members of their families who had participated in the sin of intermarriage. The list of these leaders is not provided, a somewhat peculiar oversight in a book noted for its fondness for lists. These leaders and the guilty parties would travel to Jerusalem to have their situation investigated by the national leadership who would then offer their decision. It can be assumed that there were probably some occasions where the accused were found to be innocent. The proceedings took three months, thus revealing how deeply this sin permeated the community. Assuming the list is complete, a total of 113 Jews had married foreign women.

The List of Those Guilty of Intermarriage (10:18-44)

The list begins with a roster of the religious leaders who were guilty of intermarriage. The roster includes 16 priests and 10 Levites, together comprising almost one-fourth of the total. The priests are listed first, revealing that the sin reached even to the highest ranks of the spiritual leaders. In fact, the family of the high priest begins the list. Clearly, there was no attempt by Ezra to suppress the guilt of his fellow priests. Kidner comments,

Where we might have expected some cover-up of priestly guilt, this catalogue goes out of its way to give it prominence, with true biblical candor, by reversing the order followed in chapter 2. There it was the lay Israelites who were enumerated first; here it is their spiritual leaders, headed by descendants of the honored high priest Jeshua-ben-Jozadak (cf. 3:2; 5:2, etc.). Clearly neither ancestry nor office can be a guarantee of moral probity.[3]

The priests guilty of the sin of intermarriage made a pledge to put away their wives. The phrase "they pledged" is literally "they gave their hands," a common way of confirming an agreement (cf. 2 Kin. 10:15; Ezek. 17:18). This gesture was probably similar to our modern handshake. These priests also offered a ram as a guilt offering for their offense. This guilt offering is prescribed even if the offender was unaware of the transgression (cf. Lev 5:17-19). Ignorance does not equal innocence. The offender is still viewed as guilty and in need of expiation. Even though the pledge and offering are mentioned only in this verse, it can be assumed that everyone who was guilty of this offense probably took the same steps. Verse 24 identifies one singer and three gatekeepers. For more information on these guilds see the comments on 2:40-42. Interestingly enough, there is no mention of the temple servants engaging in this sin.

The list continues with a roster of the laity who were guilty of intermarriage. The phrase "of Israel" separates verses 25-43 from 18-24, thereby signifying that the laity is now being addressed. The only significant item of note in this list is the problem of the wording of verse 38. The NASB follows the Masoretic Text and has "Bani, Binnui, and Shimei." Virtually all modern scholars adjust the vowels with the resultant reading "from the descendants of Binnui," a reading supported by 1 Esdras 9:34.[4] It is impossible to make a firm decision on this problem. There is no further hard evidence on either side. Williamson, however, does offer the comment, "without this emendation, the list of the family of Bani (v. 34) would be disproportionately long."[5] One other possible problem is the repetition of names. However, due to the common custom among the Jews of naming sons after ancestors, this repetition should not cause concern. We must accept the text as it stands.

Verse 44 concludes the book, identifying why the list of 18-43 is provided, that is, because all of these individuals were guilty of the sin of intermarriage with foreign women. The phrasing of the latter part of verse 44 is somewhat problematic. The Hebrew text literally reads, "and there are of them women, and they (masculine) appointed sons." Almost all modern translations rely on the phrasing provided in 1 Esdras 9:36, "and they put them away together with their children" (NRSV). This rendering shows that the community adopted the policy proposed in 10:3 (i.e., "to put away all the wives and their children").

There are no women included in this list. It is possible that no Jewish woman married a foreigner. However, the command of Nehemiah "you shall not give your daughters to their sons" (Neh. 13:25) given less than twenty years later indicates that the practice seems to have been at least known, if not common, in his day. It is more likely that the command did not apply to Jewish women since they were not permitted to divorce their husbands.

Nothing is said concerning what was done for the victims of these divorces. They would almost certainly have returned to the homes of their father. Perhaps they would remarry. Perhaps they would have lived as widows. Clearly, this would have been a traumatic situation for them and especially for their children. Although the actions of the Jews in this chapter might seem harsh to the modern reader, they were done to ensure the stability of the remnant. Hamilton explains,

Some modern readers may be quick to dismiss Ezra (and Nehemiah) as too harsh, too unrealistic, too legalistic, too racist, too xenophobic, and maybe too misogynistic. But recall that Ezra is part of a chastened community that has lost all sense of cohesion and stability, a community that is just starting to get back on its feet and learn from its earlier mistakes. Things like unrestrained intermarriage would not simply dilute the community's religious boundaries, but be a Trojan horse that would unleash a torrent of problems to compound the ones already present. If the religious heritage of the Hebrew people cannot be maintained and observed at this level—the family as the foundation of society—can it be maintained at all?[6]

The book ends rather abruptly. As Brown notes, "The narrator seems to walk off stage with the last of the women and children, leaving the reader contemplating the significance of the final scene."[7]

Ezra's reforms did not last long. Nehemiah 13:23-28 reveals that the apostasy was present when Nehemiah returned from his trip to Babylon somewhere around 430 B.C., roughly thirty years after the reforms of Ezra. The practice seems to have been uncommon in New Testament times, perhaps due to the separatistic teachings of the Pharisees.

Study Questions
1. Where do the exiles congregate at the beginning of this passage? Why?
2. Why are the people trembling?
3. What are the four key elements of Ezra's speech?
4. How do you reconcile the commands of Ezra with the words of Malachi?
5. Should Christians divorce their unbelieving spouses today? Why or why not?

6. What is the response of the assembly to the speech of Ezra?
7. Why are some of the people opposed to the agreement?
8. Do you think that those guilty of intermarriage should have divorced their foreign wives? Why or why not?
9. In your opinion, why does Ezra record the names of the guilty parties?
10. What has the book of Ezra taught you about God?

NOTES

Foreword

1. M. S. Terry, *Biblical Hermeneutics: A Treatise on the Interpretation of the Old and New Testaments* (1885, reprint, Grand Rapids: Zondervan Publishing House, 1947), 600.
2. Roy B. Zuck, *Basic Bible Interpretation* (Colorado Springs: Victor, 1991), 100.

Introduction

1. Eskenazi writes, "the fact that the MT [Masoretic Text] transmits Ezra-Nehemiah as a single, unified book *decisively* [my emphasis] establishes the perimeters of the book" (Tamara C. Eskenazi, *In an Age of Prose: A Literary Approach to Ezra-Nehemiah*, The Society of Biblical Literature Monograph Series, ed. Adela Yarbro Collins, no. 36 [Atlanta, GA: Scholars Press, 1988], 11).
2. It should be noted, however, that another rabbinical decision contradicts this statement (*Sanhedrin* 93b). In this passage the rabbis assert that Nehemiah was the author of the entire work.

3. For a notable example of such a study, see Eskenazi, *In an Age of Prose*, 37ff.

4. Dorsey writes, "structural analysis strongly supports the compositional unity of these two books. That the two books together have seven parts would by itself support their unity. The interlacing parallel and symmetric structuring schemes that tie the two books together seem to seal the argument" (David A. Dorsey, *The Literary Structure of the Old Testament* [Grand Rapids: Baker Books, 1999], 160). Eskenazi adds, "The complexity of Ezra-Nehemiah gains coherence when one looks at the book's distinctive structure and discerns its major themes" (Eskenazi, *In an Age of Prose*, 37). She goes on to argue that the repeated list of returnees in Ezra 2 and Nehemiah 7 is the key to the structure of the book and serves to unify the work (ibid., 37ff.).

5. David J. A. Clines, *Ezra, Nehemiah, Esther*, New Century Bible Commentary, ed. Ronald E. Clements and Matthew Black (Grand Rapids: William B. Eerdmans Publishing Company, 1984), 228; Joseph Blenkinsopp, *Ezra-Nehemiah*, Old Testament Library, ed. Peter Ackroyd, James Barr, Bernhard W. Anderson, and James L. Mays (Philadelphia: Westminster Press, 1988), 47; Sara Japhet, "Composition and Chronology in the Book of Ezra-Nehemiah," in *Second Temple Studies: 2. Temple Community in the Persian Period*, ed. Tamara C. Eskenazi and Kent H. Richards. Journal for the Study of the Old Testament Supplement Series, ed. David J. A. Clines and Philip R. Davies, no. 175 (Sheffield: JSOT Press, 1994), 193.

6. R. K. Harrison, *Introduction to the Old Testament* (Grand Rapids: William B. Eerdmans Publishing Company, 1969), 1146. Harrison concludes his thoughts on the authorship of Nehemiah by stating "in considering Nehemiah as a whole, there seem to be only highly subjective reasons for not regarding this work as the autobiography of the renowned civil governor of Judaea" (ibid.).

7. Eskenazi disagrees, asserting that the repeated list is the clue to the structure of the Book of Ezra-Nehemiah. She explains, "because Ezra 2 through Nehemiah 7 constitutes ultimately a single event, the grand celebration does not take place after the completion of the Temple in Ezra 6 but awaits and comes only after the completion of the whole project. At that time the completed house of God, Temple, people, walls, are sanctified (Neh. 12:30). Hence, according to Ezra-Nehemiah's structure, all of these developments between Ezra 2 and Nehemiah 7 are necessary elements of the full realization of Cyrus's decree. Only when they have been executed can the great fanfare of the dedication proper take place. Nehemiah 8-13 is that dedication. The repetition of the list is thus the key to Ezra-Nehemiah's structure" (Tamara C. Eskenazi, "The Structure of Ezra-Nehemiah and the Integrity of the Book," *Journal of Biblical Literature* 107 [December 1988]: 647). She also supplies six reasons why the repeated list is foundational to the Book of Ezra-Nehemiah: First, the repeated list unifies the material. Second, the repeated list indicates emphasis. Third, the repeated list expresses Ezra-Nehemiah's view of the wholeness of the people. Fourth, the repeated list bridges past and present. Fifth, the repeated list suggests the broadening of communal participation. And finally, the repeated list implies that the list sets equivalencies between Torah reading and sacrifices (ibid., 646-50). Dorsey agrees that the repeated list is a key to the structure of the unified books. He writes, "the puzzling repetition of the list of returnees under Zerubbabel (Ezra 2; Neh. 7) functions structurally to connect the beginning and end of the work and to reinforce its symmetric design (and to draw attention to the importance of the people who returned" (Dorsey, *The Literary Structure of the Old Testament*, 160-61).

8. Edward J. Young, *An Introduction to the Old Testament* (Grand Rapids: William B. Eerdmans Publishing Company, 1964), 378.

9. James C. VanderKam, "Ezra-Nehemiah or Ezra and Nehemiah?" in *Priests, Prophets and Scribes*, ed. Eugene Ulrich, John W. Wright, Robert P. Carroll, and Philip R. Davies. Journal for the Study of the Old Testament Supplement Series, ed. David J. A. Clines and Philip R. Davies, no. 149 (Sheffield: JSOT Press, 1992), 67-68.

10. David Kraemer, "On the Relationship of the Books of Ezra and Nehemiah," *Journal for the Study of the Old Testament* 59 (September 1993): 84.

11. Ibid., 82.

12. Ibid., 83.

13. One such example is Eskenazi, *In an Age of Prose*, 41ff.

14. For a notable example of such a treatment, see Charles R. Swindoll, *Hand Me Another Brick,* rev. ed. (Nashville: Word Publishing, 1990).

15. David Kraemer, "On the Relationship of the Books of Ezra and Nehemiah," 76.

Chapter 1

1. Many scholars have advanced the view that Gubaru is to be identified as the "Darius the Mede" figure referenced in the Book of Daniel (e.g., 5:31; 6:9, 25, 28; 9:1). Howard maintains, "The details of 'Darius the Mede's' life fit those of Gaubaruwa [Gubaru] very closely, and 'Darius the Mede' may simply have been an alternate title for him" (David M. Howard, Jr., *An Introduction to the Old Testament Historical Books* [Chicago: Moody Press, 1993], 285. For a full explanation of this view, see W. H. Shea, "Darius the Mede: An Update," *Andrews University Seminary Studies* 20 (autumn 1982): 229-48. An alternative view identifies Cyrus II as "Darius the Mede." According to this view, the last portion of Daniel 6:28, "So Daniel prospered during the reign of Darius and the reign of Cyrus the Persian," should be understood to mean "the reign of Darius, that is, the reign of Cyrus" (see

NIV margin note). For a full explanation of this view, see
B. E. Colless, "Cyrus the Persian as Darius the Mede in the
Book of Daniel," *Journal for the Study of the Old Testament*
56 (December 1992): 113-26.
2. For a full listing of these battles and their dates, see Edwin
M. Yamauchi, *Persia and the Bible* (Grand Rapids: Baker
Books, 1990), 146.
3. Eugene H. Merrill, *Kingdom of Priests* (Grand Rapids:
Baker Books, 1987), 498.
4. Edwin M. Yamauchi, "The Archaeological Background
of Nehemiah," *Bibliotheca Sacra* 137 (October-December
1980): 291.

Chapter 2
1. Edwin M. Yamauchi, "Persians," in *Peoples of the Old
Testament World*, ed. Edward J. Hoerth, Gerald D. Mattingly,
and Edwin M. Yamauchi (Grand Rapids: Baker Books,
1994), 110.
2. Ibid.
3. David M. Howard, Jr., *An Introduction to the Old Testament
Historical Books* (Chicago: Moody Press, 1993), 285.
4. Leslie C. Allen, "Ezra," in *Ezra, Nehemiah, Esther*,
New International Biblical Commentary (Peabody, MA:
Hendrickson Publishers, Inc., 2003), 15-16.
5. Richard T. Hallock, *Persepolis Fortification Tablets*
(Chicago: University of Chicago, 1969), 6.

Chapter 3
1. H. G. M. Williamson, *Ezra, Nehemiah*, Word Biblical
Commentary (Waco, TX: Word Books, 1985), 11.
2. The city of Jerusalem had been conquered by the Israelites
by the time of the Judges, however, it does not seem to have
been occupied by the Hebrews (cf. Judg 1:8). It is not until

King David conquers the city and builds himself a palace there that Jerusalem is made the capital of the nation (2 Sam. 5:6-12).
3. F. Charles Fensham, *The Books of Ezra and Nehemiah*, New International Commentary on the Old Testament, ed. R. K. Harrison (Grand Rapids: William B. Eerdmans Publishing Company, 1982), 10.
4. Edwin M. Yamauchi, "The Archaeological Background of Ezra," *Bibliotheca Sacra* 137 (July-September 1980): 201.
5. Scholars differ greatly on the date of Zoroaster. Mary Boyce argues for a date prior to 1200 B.C. (Mary Boyce, *A History of Zoroastrianism* [Leiden: Brill, 1975], 1:216-17) while Yamauchi hold a date in the ninth or tenth century B.C. (Edwin M. Yamauchi, "Persians," in *Peoples of the Old Testament World*, ed. Edward J. Hoerth, Gerald D. Mattingly, and Edwin M. Yamauchi [Grand Rapids: Baker Books, 1994], 122).
6. Joseph Blenkinsopp, "Temple and Society in Achaemenid Judah," in *Second Temple Studies: 1. Persian Period*, ed. Philip R. Davies, Journal for the Study of the Old Testament Supplement Series, ed. David J. A. Clines and Philip R. Davies, no. 117 (Sheffield: JSOT Press, 1991), 24.
7. R. de Vaux, "The Decrees of Cyrus and Darius on the Rebuilding of the Temple," in *The Bible and the Ancient Near East* (London: Darton, Longman & Todd, 1971), 77-78.
8. Blenkinsopp, "Temple and Society in Achaemenid Judah," 26.
9. Joseph Blenkinsopp, *Ezra-Nehemiah*, Old Testament Library, ed. Peter Ackroyd, James Barr, Bernhard W. Anderson, and James L. Mays (Philadelphia: Westminster Press, 1988), 66-67.
10. Leslie C. Allen, "Ezra," in *Ezra, Nehemiah, Esther*, New International Biblical Commentary (Peabody, MA: Hendrickson Publishers, Inc., 2003), 17. For a full description of the Exodus imagery in Ezra see Melody D. Knowles,

"Pilgrimage Imagery in the Returns in Ezra," *Journal of Biblical Literature* 123 (March 2004): 57-74.
11. Fensham, *The Books of Ezra and Nehemiah*, 44.
12. Williamson, *Ezra, Nehemiah*, 14.

Chapter 5
1. Allen is among those who hold to two returns. See Leslie C. Allen, "Ezra," in *Ezra, Nehemiah, Esther*, New International Biblical Commentary (Peabody, MA: Hendrickson Publishers, Inc., 2003), 23-24.
2. H. L. Allrik, "The Lists of Zerubbabel (Nehemiah 7 and Ezra 2) and the Hebrew Numeral Notation," *Bulletin of the American Schools of Oriental Research* 136 (December 1954): 21-27.
3. S. Japhet, "Sheshbazzar and Zerubbabel," *Zeitschrift für die alttestamentliche Wissenschaft* 94, no. 1 (1982): 76.

Chapter 7
1. H. G. M. Williamson, *Ezra, Nehemiah*, Word Biblical Commentary (Waco, TX: Word Books, 1985), 46.

Chapter 8
1. Merrill F. Unger, *Unger's Bible Dictionary*, 3d ed. (Chicago: Moody Press, 1966), 1121.
2. F. Charles Fensham, *The Books of Ezra and Nehemiah*, New International Commentary on the Old Testament, ed. R. K. Harrison (Grand Rapids: William B. Eerdmans Publishing Company, 1982), 62-63.
3. Leslie C. Allen, "Ezra," in *Ezra, Nehemiah, Esther*, New International Biblical Commentary (Peabody, MA: Hendrickson Publishers, Inc., 2003), 32.

Chapter 9
1. William F. Albright, *The Biblical Period from Abraham to Ezra*, 2d ed. (New York: Harper & Brothers Publishers, 1963), 87.
2. Alon lists three Rabbinic views concerning the origins of the Samaritans. First, the prevailing view regarded the Samaritans as the descendants of those people who were settled in Eretz-Israel by the Assyrian kings, in accordance with the Biblical tradition. This view is supported by Josephus, who calls them Cutheans and attests that they were aliens who were brought to the country by the king of Assyria, denying their relationship to the House of Joseph (*Antiquities* 9.14.3; 11.8.6; 12.5.5). Second, another tradition regarded the Samaritans as primarily of Cuthean origin, except that the Jews had intermingled with them (*Qiddushin* 4.3). Third, yet another tradition regarded the Samaritans as the product of the intermingling of Israelites with proselytes (*Tractate Kuthim* 2.7). For an extensive review of the evidence, see Gedalyahu Alon, *Jews, Judaism and the Classical World*, trans. Israel Abrahams (Jerusalem: Magnes Press, The Hebrew University, 1977), 354-73. The Samaritans themselves claim that they are the direct descendants of a faithful nucleus of ancient Israel. They trace Israel's apostasy to the eleventh century B.C. when the cultic center was moved from Gerizim to Shiloh (and eventually Jerusalem). Thus, they do not see themselves as the remnant of the old northern kingdom of Israel, but as a separate group alongside them. For a full treatment of the historical origins of the Samaritans, see Hugh G. M. Williamson, "Samaritans," in *Dictionary of Jesus and the Gospels*, ed. Joel B. Green, Scot McKnight, and I. Howard Marshall (Downers Grove, IL: InterVarsity Press, 1992), 725-27.
3. The Samaritans were not alone in separating from the orthodox Jewish populace and developing a syncretistic Jewish-pagan religion. The Elephantine papyri describe a

Jewish settlement on a small island in the Nile, at present-day Aswan, near the southern Egyptian border. The papyri reveal the existence of a temple dedicated to Yahweh. One of the most interesting letters, addressed from the colonists to Bagoas, the Persian governor of Judea, in 407 B.C. (Pritchard, *Ancient Near Eastern Texts Relating to the Old Testament*, 492), speaks of the destruction of this temple and mentions requests for help made to the two sons of Sanballat, governor of Samaria. Howard writes, "The temple at Elephantine is an example of syncretistic Jewish practice at this time, which incorporated elements of pagan worship along with true worship" (David M. Howard, Jr., *An Introduction to the Old Testament Historical Books* [Chicago: Moody Press, 1993], 289).

4. H. G. M. Williamson, *Ezra, Nehemiah*, Word Biblical Commentary (Waco, TX: Word Books, 1985), 50.

Chapter 10

1. Dozeman comments on this phrase, "The author of Ezra-Nehemiah employs the geopolitical meaning of *Abar Naharah* [beyond the river] to advance three social and religious arguments about the nature of Persian rule and its impact on Yahwism. First, the Persian monarchs in general, and Artaxerxes in particular, are idealized as kings who uphold the law in *Abar Naharah* and are restricted by it. Second, not only Persian kings but Persian law itself is represented as an ideal in Ezra-Nehemiah. It is impartial and equally binding for Persians and Judeans. Third, the author of Ezra-Nehemiah advocates a form of environmental determinism in the region of *Abar Naharah*. The Persian rule of law in *Abar Naharah* provides the environment (i.e., the *nomos*) for the transformation of Yahwism from a messianic religion centered in a monarchy to a religion of law, constituted in the Torah of Moses" (Thomas B. Dozeman, "Geography and

History in Herodotus and in Ezra-Nehemiah," *Journal of Biblical Literature* 122 [July 2003]: 459).

Chapter 11
1. F. Charles Fensham, *The Books of Ezra and Nehemiah*, New International Commentary on the Old Testament, ed. R. K. Harrison (Grand Rapids: William B. Eerdmans Publishing Company, 1982), 80.
2. Derek Kidner, *Ezra and Nehemiah*, Tyndale Old Testament Commentaries (Downers Grove, IL: InterVarsity Press, 1979), 54.
3. Williamson adds, "Perhaps the expression was intended to suggest a contrast with the Persian inspectors. These were known popularly as 'the king's eye,' and must have been regarded as somewhat threatening and sinister. The biblical author knows, however of One whose care overrides even their potential menace" (H. G. M. Williamson, *Ezra, Nehemiah*, Word Biblical Commentary [Waco, TX: Word Books, 1985], 77).

Chapter 12
1. Derek Kidner, *Ezra and Nehemiah*, Tyndale Old Testament Commentaries (Downers Grove, IL: InterVarsity Press, 1979), 55.
2. James B. Pritchard, ed., *Ancient Near Eastern Texts Relating to the Old Testament*, 3d ed. (Princeton: Princeton University Press, 1969), 316.
3. Leslie C. Allen, "Ezra," in *Ezra, Nehemiah, Esther*, New International Biblical Commentary (Peabody, MA: Hendrickson Publishers, Inc., 2003), 45.

Chapter 13
1. For a full discussion of the relationship between these two documents, see E. J. Bickerman, "The Edict of Cyrus in Ezra 1," *Journal of Biblical Literature* 65 (1946): 259-275.
2. This is the view held by Williamson (H. G. M. Williamson, *Ezra, Nehemiah*, Word Biblical Commentary [Waco, TX: Word Books, 1985], 83).
3. F. Charles Fensham, *The Books of Ezra and Nehemiah*, New International Commentary on the Old Testament, ed. R. K. Harrison (Grand Rapids: William B. Eerdmans Publishing Company, 1982), 91.

Chapter 14
1. Joseph Blenkinsopp, "Temple and Society in Achaemenid Judah," in *Second Temple Studies: 1. Persian Period*, ed. Philip R. Davies, Journal for the Study of the Old Testament Supplement Series, ed. David J. A. Clines and Philip R. Davies, no. 117 (Sheffield: JSOT Press, 1991), 37.
2. Joseph Blenkinsopp, *Ezra-Nehemiah*, Old Testament Library, ed. Peter Ackroyd, James Barr, Bernhard W. Anderson, and James L. Mays (Philadelphia: Westminster Press, 1988), 68.
3. Ibid., 69.

Chapter 15
1. F. Charles Fensham, *The Books of Ezra and Nehemiah*, New International Commentary on the Old Testament, ed. R. K. Harrison (Grand Rapids: William B. Eerdmans Publishing Company, 1982), 8-9.
2. Ibid., 99.
3. Derek Kidner, *Ezra and Nehemiah*, Tyndale Old Testament Commentaries (Downers Grove, IL: InterVarsity Press, 1979), 62.

Chapter 16

1. Othniel Margalith, "The Political Role of Ezra as Persian Governor," *Zeitschrift für die Alttestamentliche Wissenschaft* 98:1 (1986): 111.

2. Derek Kidner, *Ezra and Nehemiah*, Tyndale Old Testament Commentaries (Downers Grove, IL: InterVarsity Press, 1979), 18-19.

3. P. R. Ackroyd, *I and II Chronicles, Ezra, Nehemiah*, Torch Bible (London: SCM Press, 1973).

Chapter 17

1. R. A. Bowman, "The Book of Ezra and the Book of Nehemiah," in *The Interpreter's Bible* (Nashville: Abingdon Publishers, 1954), 3:632.

2. F. Charles Fensham, *The Books of Ezra and Nehemiah*, New International Commentary on the Old Testament, ed. R. K. Harrison (Grand Rapids: William B. Eerdmans Publishing Company, 1982), 117.

Chapter 18

1. Some scholars believe that the "foreign women" and "the peoples of the lands" were actually Jews who were not deported under Nebuchadnezzar but remained in the land during the exile. For a full explanation of this view, see L. Smith-Christopher, "The Mixed Marriage Crisis in Ezra 9-10 and Nehemiah 13: A Study of the Sociology of the Post-Exilic Judaean Community," in *Second Temple Studies: 2. Temple Community in the Persian Period*, ed. Tamara C. Eskenazi and Kent H. Richards (Sheffield: Sheffield Academic, 1994): 243-65.

2. Keith N. Schoville, "Canaanites and Amorites," in *Peoples of the Old Testament World*, ed. Alfred J. Hoerth, Gerald L.

Mattingly, and Edwin M. Yamauchi (Grand Rapids: Baker Books, 1974), 178.

3. Merrill F. Unger, *Unger's Bible Dictionary* (Chicago: Moody Press, 1966), 493.

4. Gerald L. Mattingly, "Moabites," in *Peoples of the Old Testament World*, ed. Alfred J. Hoerth, Gerald L. Mattingly, and Edwin M. Yamauchi (Grand Rapids: Baker Books, 1974), 320.

5. James K. Hoffmeier, "Egyptians," in *Peoples of the Old Testament World*, ed. Alfred J. Hoerth, Gerald L. Mattingly, and Edwin M. Yamauchi (Grand Rapids: Baker Books, 1974), 283.

6. F. Charles Fensham, *The Books of Ezra and Nehemiah*, New International Commentary on the Old Testament, ed. R. K. Harrison (Grand Rapids: William B. Eerdmans Publishing Company, 1982), 124.

7. Brown writes, "Holiness is more important than even the closest of human relationships: marriage. Although divorce is hateful to God, this episode reinforces the principle taught in Deuteronomy 13 that unswerving loyalty to Yahweh is of far greater importance than the continuance of marriage. The Lord regards His people's relationship to Himself as the preeminent priority of their lives" (A. Philip Brown II, "The Problem of Mixed Marriages in Ezra 9-10," *Bibliotheca Sacra* 162 [October-December 2005]: 458).

8. Dow Marmur, *Intermarriage* (London: Reform Synagogues of Great Britain, 1978), 2.

Chapter 19
1. Frederic Bush, *Ruth, Esther*, Word Biblical Commentary (Dallas: Word Books, 1996), 133.

2. F. Charles Fensham, *The Books of Ezra and Nehemiah*, New International Commentary on the Old Testament, ed. R.

K. Harrison (Grand Rapids: William B. Eerdmans Publishing Company, 1982), 129.

3. H. G. M. Williamson, *Ezra, Nehemiah*, Word Biblical Commentary (Waco, TX: Word Books, 1985), 136.

4. Ibid.

Chapter 20

1. H. G. M. Williamson, *Ezra, Nehemiah*, Word Biblical Commentary (Waco, TX: Word Books, 1985), 149.

2. Brown believes the shift occurs to highlight the shared responsibility for the divorces amongst the various groups that supported the decision. He writes, "The third-person narration distances readers from Ezra and the events immediately surrounding him, creating a sense of a more objective point of view. . . . This method of presentation makes it clear that though Ezra was at the center of things, he was not the one making them happen. In fact the procedure and penalty for dealing with the issue was agreed on first by the priests, the Levites, and all Israel, and was then confirmed by the entire male population of Judah and Benjamin (10:2-14), and was finally executed by committees in each city (v. 16)" (A. Philip Brown II, "Point of View in the Book of Ezra," *Bibliotheca Sacra* 162 [July-September 2005]: 323-24.

3. F. Charles Fensham, *The Books of Ezra and Nehemiah*, New International Commentary on the Old Testament, ed. R. K. Harrison (Grand Rapids: William B. Eerdmans Publishing Company, 1982), 135.

4. Ibid.

5. Ibid., 138.

Chapter 21
1. John A. Martin, "Ezra," in *The Bible Knowledge Commentary, Old Testament*, ed. John F. Walvoord and Roy B. Zuck (Colorado Springs: Victor Books, 1985), 671.
2. Ibid.
3. Derek Kidner, *Ezra and Nehemiah*, Tyndale Old Testament Commentaries (Downers Grove, IL: InterVarsity Press, 1979), 72.
4. F. Charles Fensham, *The Books of Ezra and Nehemiah*, New International Commentary on the Old Testament, ed. R. K. Harrison (Grand Rapids: William B. Eerdmans Publishing Company, 1982), 144.
5. H. G. M. Williamson, *Ezra, Nehemiah*, Word Biblical Commentary (Waco, TX: Word Books, 1985), 144.
6. Victor P. Hamilton, *Handbook on the Historical Books* (Grand Rapids: Baker Academic, 2004), 519.
7. A. Philip Brown II, "Nehemiah and Narrative Order in the Book of Ezra," *Bibliotheca Sacra* 162 (April-June 2005): 192.

BIBLIOGRAPHY

———∞∞∞———

Ackroyd, Peter R. *I & II Chronicles, Ezra, Nehemiah*. Torch Bible Commentaries, ed. John Marsh and Alan Richardson. London: SCM Press, Ltd., 1973.

Aharoni, Yohanan, *The Land of the Bible: A Historical Geography*. Rev. ed. Translated by A. F. Rainey. Philadelphia: Westminster Press, 1979.

Albright, William F. *The Biblical Period from Abraham to Ezra*. 2d ed. New York: Harper & Brothers Publishers, 1963.

Allen, Leslie C., and Timothy S. Laniak. *Ezra, Nehemiah, Esther*. New International Biblical Commentary. Peabody, MS: Hendrickson Publishers, 2003.

Allrik, H. L. "The Lists of Zerubbabel (Nehemiah 7 and Ezra 2) and the Hebrew Numeral Notation." *Bulletin of the American Schools of Oriental Research* 136 (December 1954): 21-27.

Alon, Gedalyahu *Jews, Judaism and the Classical World*. Translated by Israel Abrahams. Jerusalem: Magnes Press, The Hebrew University, 1977.

Archer, Gleason L. *A Survey of Old Testament Introduction*. Rev. ed. Chicago: Moody Press, 1994.

Batten, L. W. A. *A Critical and Exegetical Commentary on the Books of Ezra and Nehemiah*. International Critical Commentary. New York: Charles Scribner's Sons, 1913.

Bickerman, E. J., "The Edict of Cyrus in Ezra 1," *Journal of Biblical Literature* 65 (1946): 247-75.

Blenkinsopp, Joseph. *Ezra-Nehemiah*. Old Testament Library, ed. Peter Ackroyd, James Barr, Bernhard W. Anderson, and James L. Mays. Philadelphia: Westminster Press, 1988.

Bowman, R. A. "The Book of Ezra and the Book of Nehemiah." In *The Interpreter's Bible*. Nashville: Abingdon Publishers, 1954.

Boyce, Mary. *A History of Zoroastrianism*. Leiden: Brill, 1975.

Braun, Roddy L. "Chronicles, Ezra, and Nehemiah: Theology and Literary History." In *Studies in the Historical Books of the Old Testament*. Vetus Testamentum Supplement, ed. J. A. Emerton, no. 30, 52-64. Leiden: E. J. Brill, 1979.

Brown, A. Philip, II. "Nehemiah and Narrative Order in the Book of Ezra." *Bibliotheca Sacra* 162 (April-June 2005): 175-94.

_____. "Point of View in the Book of Ezra." *Bibliotheca Sacra* 162 (July-September 2005): 310-30.

_____. "The Problem of Mixed Marriages in Ezra 9-10." *Bibliotheca Sacra* 162 (October-December 2005): 437-58.

Clines, David J. A. *Ezra, Nehemiah, Esther*. New Century Bible Commentary, ed. Ronald E. Clements and Matthew Black. Grand Rapids: William B. Eerdmans Publishing Company, 1984.

Colless, B. E. "Cyrus the Persian as Darius the Mede in the Book of Daniel." *Journal for the Study of the Old Testament* 56 (December 1992): 113-26.

Cross, Frank Moore, Jr. "A Reconstruction of the Judean Restoration." *Journal of Biblical Literature* 94 (March 1975): 4-18.

Davies, Philip R., ed. *Second Temple Studies: 1. Persian Period.* Journal for the Study of the Old Testament Supplement Series, ed. David J. A. Clines and Philip R. Davies, no. 117. Sheffield: JSOT Press, 1991.

Dillard, Raymond B., and Tremper Longman, III. *An Introduction to the Old Testament.* Grand Rapids: Zondervan Publishing House, 1994.

Dorsey, David A. *The Literary Structure of the Old Testament.* Grand Rapids: Baker Books, 1999.

Dozeman, Thomas B. "Geography and History in Herodotus and in Ezra-Nehemiah." *Journal of Biblical Literature* 122 (September 2003): 449-66.

Driver, S. R. *An Introduction to the Literature of the Old Testament.* 9th ed. New York: Charles Scribner's Sons, 1913.

Eskenazi, Tamara C. *In an Age of Prose: A Literary Approach to Ezra-Nehemiah.* The Society of Biblical Literature Monograph Series, ed. Adela Yarbro Collins, no. 36. Atlanta, GA: Scholars Press, 1988.

————. "The Structure of Ezra-Nehemiah and the Integrity of the Book." *Journal of Biblical Literature* 107 (December 1988): 641-56.

Fensham, F. Charles. *The Books of Ezra and Nehemiah.* New International Commentary on the Old Testament, ed. R. K. Harrison. Grand Rapids: William B. Eerdmans Publishing Company, 1982.

Geisler, Norman L. and William E. Nix. *A General Introduction to the Bible.* Rev. Ed. Chicago: Moody Press, 1986.

Gowan, D. E. *Bridge Between the Testaments.* Pittsburgh: Pickwick, 1976.

Hallock, Richard T. *Persepolis Fortification Tablets.* Chicago: University of Chicago, 1969.

Hamilton, Victor P. *Handbook on the Historical Books.* Grand Rapids: Baker Academic, 2004.

Harrison, R. K. *Introduction to the Old Testament.* Grand Rapids: William B. Eerdmans Publishing Company, 1969.

Hoerth, Edward J., Gerald D. Mattingly, and Edwin M. Yamauchi, eds. *Peoples of the Old Testament World.* Grand Rapids: Baker Books, 1994.

Holmgren, Fredrick Carlson. *Israel Alive Again: A Commentary on the Books of Ezra and Nehemiah.* International Theological Commentary, ed. George A. F. Knight and Fredrick Carlson Holmgren. Grand Rapids: William B. Eerdmans Publishing Company, 1987.

Howard, Jr., David M. *An Introduction to the Old Testament Historical Books.* Chicago: Moody Press, 1993.

In der Smitten, T. W. "Die Gründe für die Aufnahme der Nehemiaschrift in das chronistische Geschichtswerk." *Biblische Zeitschrift* 16, no. 2 (1972): 207-21.

_____. *Esra—Quellen, Überlieferung, und Geschichte.* Studia Semitica Neerlandica, no. 15. Assen: Van Gorcum, 1973.

Japhet, Sara. "Sheshbazzar and Zerubbabel." *Zeitschrift für die alttestamentliche Wissenschaft* 94, no. 1 (1982): 66-98.

Kellermann, U. *Nehemia—Quellen, Überlieferung, und Geschichte.* Beihefte zur Zeitschrift für die alttestamentliche Wissenschaft, ed. Georg Fohrer, vol. 102. Berlin: Töpelmann, 1967.

Kenyon, Kathleen. *Jerusalem.* London: Thames & Hudson, 1967.

Kidner, Derek. *Ezra and Nehemiah*. The Tyndale Old Testament Commentaries, ed. D. J. Wiseman. Downers Grove, IL: InterVarsity Press, 1979.

Knowles, Melody D. "Pilgrimage Imagery in the Returns in Ezra." *Journal of Biblical Literature* 123 (March 2004): 57-74.

Kraemer, David. "On the Relationship of the Books of Ezra and Nehemiah." *Journal for the Study of the Old Testament* 59 (September 1993): 73-92.

Loken, Israel. "A literary Analysis of Nehemiah." Ph.D. diss., Dallas Theological Seminary, 2001.

Marmur, Dow. *Intermarriage*. London: Reform Synagogues of Great Britain, 1978.

Martin, John A. "Ezra." In *The Bible Knowledge Commentary, Old Testament*, ed. John F. Walvoord and Roy B. Zuck, 651-72. Colorado Springs: Victor Books, 1985.

Merrill, Eugene H. *Kingdom of Priests: A History of Old Testament Israel*. Grand Rapids: Baker Books, 1987.

_____. "A Theology of Ezra-Nehemiah and Esther." In *A Biblical Theology of the Old Testament*, ed. Roy B. Zuck, 189-205. Chicago: Moody Press, 1991.

Myers, Jacob M., *I and II Esdras*. Anchor Bible, ed. William F. Albright and David N. Freedman, vol. 42. Garden City, NY: Doubleday & Company, 1974.

_____. *Ezra, Nehemiah*. Anchor Bible, ed. William F. Albright and David N. Freedman, vol. 14. Garden City, NY: Doubleday & Company, 1965.

Pohlmann, K. F. *Studien zum dritten Esra*. Forschungen zur Religion und Literatur des Alten und Neuen Testaments, vol. 104. Göttingen: Vandenhoeck & Ruprecht, 1970.

Pritchard, James B., ed. *Ancient Near Eastern Texts Relating to the Old Testament.* 3d ed. Princeton: Princeton University Press, 1969.

Radmacher, Earl D., Ronald B. Allen, and H. Wayne House, ed. *Nelson's New Illustrated Bible Commentary.* Nashville: Thomas Nelson Publishers, 1999.

Reynolds, Steve L. "A Literary Analysis of Nehemiah." Ph.D. diss., Bob Jones University, 1994.

Rowley, Harold H. "Nehemiah's Mission and Its Background." *Bulletin of the John Rylands University Library of Manchester* 37 (March 1955): 528-61.

_____. "Sanballat and the Samaritan Temple." *Bulletin of the John Rylands University Library of Manchester* 38 (September 1955): 166-98.

Rudolph, W. *Esra und Nehemia.* Handbuch zum Alten Testament, ed. Otto Eissfeldt, vol. 20. Tübingen: J. C. B. Mohr, 1949.

Seume, Richard H. *Nehemiah: God's Builder.* Chicago: Moody Press, 1978.

Shea, W. H. "Darius the Mede: An Update." *Andrews University Seminary Studies* 20 (Autumn 1982): 229-48.

Smith-Christopher, L. "The Mixed Marriage Crisis in Ezra 9-10 and Nehemiah 13: A Study of the Sociology of the Post-Exilic Judaean Community." In *Second Temple Studies: 2. Temple Community in the Persian Period,* ed. Tamara C. Eskenazi and Kent H. Richards. Sheffield: Sheffield Academic, 1994.

Swindoll, Charles R. *Hand Me Another Brick.* Rev. ed. Nashville: Word Publishing, 1990.

Talmon, Shemaryahu. "Ezra and Nehemiah (Books and Men)." In *The Interpreter's Dictionary of the Bible, Supplementary Volume,* ed. Keith Crim et al., 317-28. Nashville: Abingdon Press, 1962.

Terry, M. S. *Biblical Hermeneutics: A Treatise on the Interpretation of the Old and New Testaments.* 1885. Reprint, Grand Rapids: Zondervan Publishing House, 1947.

Throntveit, Mark A. *Ezra, Nehemiah.* Interpretation, ed. James Luther Mays. Louisville: John Knox Press, 1992.

Torrey, C. C. *Ezra Studies.* Chicago: University of Chicago Press, 1910.

Ulrich, Eugene, John W. Wright, Robert P. Carroll, and Philip R. Davies, eds. *Priests, Prophets and Scribes.* Journal for the Study of the Old Testament Supplement Series, ed. David J. A. Clines and Philip R. Davies, no. 149. Sheffield: JSOT Press, 1992.

Unger, Merrill F., ed. *Unger's Bible Dictionary*, 3d ed. Chicago: Moody Press, 1966.

Vaux, R. de. *The Bible and the Ancient Near East.* London: Darton, Longman & Todd, 1971.

Walton, John H., Victor H. Matthews, and Mark W. Chavalas. *The IVP Bible Background Commentary: Old Testament.* Downer's Grove, IL: InterVarsity Press, 2000.

Welch, A. C. *Post-Exilic Judaism.* Edinburgh: Blackwood, 1935.

Whitcomb, John C. "Ezra." In *The Wycliffe Bible Commentary*, ed. Charles F. Pfeiffer and Everett F. Harrison, 423-33. Chicago: Moody Press, 1962.

Wiersbe, Warren W. *The Bible Exposition Commentary: Old Testament History.* Colorado Springs: Victor Books, 2003.

Williamson, Hugh G. M. "The Composition of Ezra i-vi." *Journal of Theological Studies* 34 (April 1983): 1-30.

_____. *Ezra, Nehemiah*. Word Biblical Commentary, ed. David A. Hubbard and Glenn W. Barker, vol. 16. Waco, TX: Word Books, Publisher, 1985.

_____. "Samaritans." In *Dictionary of Jesus and the Gospels*, ed. Joel B. Green, Scot McKnight, and I. Howard Marshall, 724-28. Downers Grove, IL: InterVarsity Press, 1992.

Yamauchi, Edwin M. "The Archaeological Background of Ezra." *Bibliotheca Sacra* 137 (July-September 1980): 195-211.

_____. "The Archaeological Background of Nehemiah." *Bibliotheca Sacra* 137 (October-December 1980): 291-309.

_____. "Ezra." In *Zondervan NIV Bible Commentary, Old Testament*, ed. Kenneth L. Barker and John R. Kohlenberger III, 680-703. Grand Rapids: Zondervan Publishing House, 1994.

_____. *Persia and the Bible*. Grand Rapids: Baker Books, 1990.

_____. "Was Nehemiah the Cupbearer a Eunuch?" *Zeitschrift für die alttestamentliche Wissenschaft* 92, no. 1 (1980): 132-42.

Young, Edward J. *An Introduction to the Old Testament*. Grand Rapids: William B. Eerdmans Publishing Company, 1964.

Zuck, Roy B. *Basic Bible Interpretation*. Colorado Springs: Victor Books, 1991,

Printed in the United States
97018LV00001B/139-501/A